BARBARA DUMOULIN / SYLVIA SIKUNDAR

CELEBRATING OUR CULTURES

Language arts activities for classroom teachers

Pembroke Publishers Limited

© 1998 Pembroke Publishers Limited
538 Hood Road
Markham, Ontario L3R 3K9 Canada
1-800-997-9807

Distributed in the U.S. by Stenhouse Publishers
431 York Street
York, Maine 03909
1-800-998-9812

Canadian Cataloguing in Publication Data

DuMoulin, Barbara
    Celebrating our cultures : language arts activities for classroom teachers

Includes biliographical references and index.
ISBN 1-55138-102-8

1. Language arts (Elementary). 2. Holidays – Study and teaching
(Elementary). I. Sikundar, Sylvia, 1945-   . II. Title.

LB1576.D84 1998   372.6'044   C98-931627-0

    Editor: Kate Revington
    Cover Design: John Zehethofer
    Cover Photography: Ajay Photographics
    Typesetting: JayTee Graphics

Printed and Bound in Canada
9 8 7 6 5 4 3 2 1

Contents

Introduction

Looking at holiday celebrations is important in itself, but here, in *Celebrating Our Cultures*, we go beyond that. Not only will students learn something about the culture in which a celebration originates, they will treat it as a springboard for language arts activities — they will celebrate language.

This book helps fill a real need. Unlike most holiday activity books, which are art-based, it focuses on language arts and creative writing. Taking a multicultural perspective, it allows teachers to help students gain a new awareness of the richness of the cultures within our society. And it provides student activity masters and ideas for busy teachers. Just before marking special days, when our time often seems too short, our workloads too great, we can reduce preparation time without impairing instruction quality.

Holidays can provide the hook to capture students' interest in creative writing. In *Celebrating Our Cultures* students will gain opportunities to develop their imaginations and sensitivity and find an outlet for self-expression. All of them, working at their own levels, will enjoy success.

The structure of this book is based on the school year, beginning in the fall and ending in early summer. When deciding which holidays to include, we considered whether the holiday was statutory, or legal; how widely celebrated it is; and how representative of a major ethnic or religious group it is.

A Multicultural Focus

We selected holidays representative of cultures that teachers may find in their classrooms or school. These holidays can be used to familiarize classes with the cultures of their fellow students. Similarly, we have picked religious festivals to reflect several of the major religions.

We mark some common North American holidays as well. For them, we have three goals:
• to expand all students' existing knowledge of the celebrations
• to provide teachers with new ideas for exploring these celebrations with their students
• to introduce these celebrations to new immigrants

Where a celebration is closely tied with a particular religion, we have explained its origin, but not focused on religious aspects. We believe that these should be taught at the teacher's discretion. Nor have we tried to provide an in-depth analysis or history of a celebration. Many books, identified under Recommended Resources, do this. Three of the best are Caroline Parry's *Let's Celebrate: Canada's Special Days; Holidays and Anniversaries of the World*, edited by Jennifer Mossman; and *Holidays, Festivals and Celebrations of the World*, by S. E. Thompson and B. Carlson.

One special feature of *Celebrating Our Cultures* is General Celebration Activities.

Some of these will allow you to enhance your class's study of a holiday, for example, adding "Words of Wisdom" to the study of Martin Luther King, Jr., Day. Or, they will address holidays not specifically covered in this book, such as "National Birthdays," "National Birthday Activities," or "Plan Your Own Celebration."

The "celebration" of each featured holiday begins with a page of notes to the teacher. Keyed to the pages that follow, these outline the activities and add information about the holiday. Some activities are presented on worksheets and others are listed in the notes to the teacher. Whether it be a familiar North American holiday, such as Thanksgiving, or the less familiar Eid ul-Fitr, study begins with an overview noting the history, traditions and symbols of the event. You can either refresh your memory with this or hand it out directly to the students. Sometimes, students may need to refer to it to complete a puzzle or other activity.

Promoting Language Skills

Celebrating Our Cultures seeks to promote language skills while allowing students to find out more about various holidays. It features crosswords, wordsearches and other word puzzles to develop vocabulary and provide fun. It offers opportunities for creative writing, including short stories and poetry, such as cinquain, haiku, concrete and partner poems. It suggests topics for research, providing organizers, and encourages brainstorming, reflection, storytelling, speech making, and drama.

We have sought to relate the activities to the nature of the holiday. For example, when celebrating Thanksgiving, students use a web to think about what they have to be thankful for; for Groundhog Day, with its lighthearted focus, they make up a strange animal using similes. We encourage the use of artwork to enhance students' writing and suggest that students demonstrate and share the knowledge learned through their work with the class.

Some Viable Teaching Strategies

In approaching the holidays, we recommend that you apply the KWL framework. Begin with what the students know, together explore what they need to learn and ask them to demonstrate in various ways what they have learned. Start with brainstorming to find out what students know about the holiday. Then read aloud the overview provided. You can also read related stories to provide background and stimulate interest. Check Recommended Resources for some titles.

Explore the vocabulary of each holiday, starting with the puzzles.

- To increase their comprehension, invite students to develop their own puzzles. Create lists of holiday words, have students draw an appropriate symbol in a large format (e.g., a kite for Korean New Year), construct a grid inside the outline and then use this to create wordsearches. Students can exchange puzzles with their partners.
- Another idea is to create word snails where the words begin at the centre then appear in ever-larger circles; encourage students to use the last letters of one word as the beginning of the next word where possible. For example: **STAR AY** .
- Invite students to develop a dictionary for each holiday. This activity could be combined with a study of dictionaries.

A variety of language arts activities that relate to holiday symbols appear throughout the book. Creating concrete poetry is one. A related activity you can readily introduce is web making. For example:

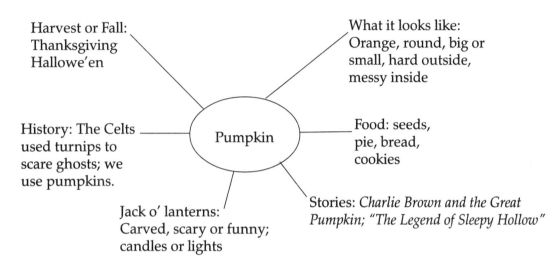

Harvest or Fall: Thanksgiving Hallowe'en

What it looks like: Orange, round, big or small, hard outside, messy inside

History: The Celts used turnips to scare ghosts; we use pumpkins.

Pumpkin

Food: seeds, pie, bread, cookies

Jack o' lanterns: Carved, scary or funny; candles or lights

Stories: *Charlie Brown and the Great Pumpkin; "The Legend of Sleepy Hollow"*

If you want to focus on syntactic, or word order, skills, ask students to create word boxes. Write the chart below on the board. Explain the five categories and ask students to generate examples. Place five labelled boxes on a table. Ask students to write a word for each category on separate pieces of paper and place these in the respective boxes. You may also add words to each box. Each student chooses a piece of paper from each box and uses the words to build a sentence.

Determiners	General Adjectives and Physical States	Proper Adjectives	Noun Modifiers	Noun
	size, shape, age, temperature, color	Nationality Brand names	Nouns used as adjectives or adjectives that are closely tied to the noun	
the	**old**	**Indian**	**clay**	**dipa**

- First, they add an adjectival phrase or clause: The old Indian clay dipa *which was filled with oil*
- Next, a verb: The old Indian clay dipa which was filled with oil *was lit.*
- Finally, an adverbial phrase: The old Indian clay dipa which was filled with oil was lit *for Diwali.*

Another strategy is to have students brainstorm verbs for each holiday. Ask students to write short sentences using these verbs. For example: My father *carves* the turkey. Write the sentences on the board and invite students to combine them into longer sentences. Or, have students take the sentences and change the verb tense. Suggest that they create poems with active verbs. Maurice Sendak does this effectively in *Where the Wild Things Are*: "They roared their terrible roars and gnashed their terrible teeth and rolled their terrible eyes and showed their terrible claws."

To set the mood or complement students' creative writing, play background music. For example, for Hallowe'en you might play "All Souls Night," from Loreena McKennitt's *The Visit*, or Camille Saint-Saens' "Dance Macabre."

For another creative writing activity, take a well-known children's song or poem and ask students to change the characters or words to fit the holiday. Then let them sing the song. This technique works for children's stories as well. "The three little pigs" could become "the three little ghosts."

You might want to split the class into groups, with each group focusing on a different activity. Later, each group can present its project so the class will gain a fuller picture of the holiday or culture — we suggest this for Passover, in particular.

Pick a holiday that will spark other events or studies. For example, lead into a school carnival by looking at Quebec's Winter Carnival. Some holidays, like Earth Day, relate well to science activities. If you want to study the Far East, use the Korean, Japanese and Chinese new years as a starting point. There are many ways to use the materials.

Working with Literary Resources

For each holiday, you will find recommended resources at the back of this book. Students may enjoy reading some of the stories or folk tales found there, and they can build upon their reading. Related activities include making a reading log, writing a book report or sociogram, devising a character description, and doing Reader's Theatre. You will find some ideas under General Holiday Activities.

In Reader's Theatre, the emphasis is on reading expressively rather than acting. Students read from scripts and use voice and tone to convey story, setting, and character. When presenting a script students can stand in a line facing the audience, with each person stepping forward when it's time to speak. Students could also sit in a curved line to read — they should be able to see one another as well as their audience. For more information about this activity, see Mildred Laughlin and Kathy Latrobe's *Readers Theatre for Children*. It has an excellent explanation as well as completed scripts of several well-known children's stories.

A sociogram provides a good way to look at character relationships. Ask the students to write the main character's name in a circle. Radiating from the circle are lines to smaller circles with the names of other significant people. If the emotion goes both ways, double arrows are used; if only one way, a single arrow indicates direction. This teaching idea applies not only to books that students may read but to legends, such as the Diwali story of Rama and Sita, and true stories, such as that of Martin Luther King, Jr., featured in the text.

We hope you find this resource full of time-saving, but meaningful, ways to share in some major celebrations.

Thanksgiving

A Harvest Festival

DATES

Second Monday in October, Canada
Last Thursday in November, United States

NATURE OF HOLIDAY

Statutory, traditional

OVERVIEW

Present the information in the student activity master on Thanksgiving. For more on the Pilgrims and their first Thanksgiving, check Recommended Resources for titles. You might build on the theme by inviting students to describe harvest festivals in other lands. Refer them to "Harvest Festival Report" which outlines some types of information they should look for. Encourage them to interview people about the festivals if possible. Students can also turn to reference books on other countries. Invite students to present and explain their project to the class.

Giving Thanks Web

This web facilitates introspection, allowing students to reflect on what makes them thankful. Instructions are provided on the student activity master. Students can also turn the ideas on the web into a paragraph or into a poem entitled "I am thankful for ..."
Extension activity: Ask the students to write a letter to someone who has helped them in some way and for whom they are thankful, perhaps the school secretary, a librarian, or a police officer. You might want to review with the students how to write a personal letter.

Thanksgiving Puzzle

Students fill in the blanks using provided clues. Here is the answer key: turkey, hay, yam, corn, pumpkin pie, scarecrow, grains, family, harvest, pioneers, cranberries, wagon.
Extension activity: Brainstorm words that are used for harvest, fall and thanksgiving. Give students an outline shape of a turkey or cornucopia. Ask them to create a wordsearch within the shape. Explain that their words can be horizontal, vertical, or diagonal and that a wordlist or clues need to be given. Have students exchange puzzles and solve them. This is an excellent partner activity, especially when students are devising clues.

Thanksgiving: *A Harvest Festival*

Many cultures have a time to celebrate the end of the growing season when all crops have been harvested for winter. The ancient Greeks, Romans, and Egyptians all celebrated at harvest time and thanked their gods and goddesses. Today, throughout the world, we still celebrate at this time. There are many names for this holiday: in Germany, it is called Martinmas; in England, Harvest Festival. In North America, it is called Thanksgiving.

Thanksgiving is a day when people get together with their families and enjoy dinners that may feature roast turkey, mashed potatoes, fall vegetables such as squash, cranberry sauce, and pumpkin pie topped with whipped cream. It is a time of giving thanks for all the good things that have happened during the year: for health, family, friends and, of course, food.

Canada and the United States celebrate Thanksgiving at different times. In Canada, it is celebrated on the second Monday in October. In the United States the holiday is much later — the last Thursday in November. In both countries it is a national holiday when few people have to work.

Celebrating Survival

In the United States, the first people to officially mark a time for thanksgiving were the Pilgrims. We often think of these pioneers as having started the celebration in 1621. However, harvest feasts were held long before that in North America. Native peoples throughout the continent harvested and preserved food to be stored for the long winter ahead and thanked their gods. In Canada, both the early French and English settlers held thanksgiving celebrations in their new land. English settlers in Newfoundland under Martin Frobisher ate a harvest celebration dinner in 1568. More than 300 years ago, French settlers, led by Samuel de Champlain, celebrated with a large dinner after struggling through a difficult first year in Nova Scotia but getting a good harvest the following year.

Regardless of the country or culture, the story is similar. People gave thanks for a successful beginning in a new land. Since then many other people have immigrated to Canada and the United States and brought their customs for giving thanks too.

Harvest Festival Report

Describe the harvest festival of a country of your choice. On a separate page or on a poster write a short report. Illustrate it with harvest scenes.

What to include:
- Name of country
- Name of festival
- Date and length of festival
- Special traditions
- Special foods
- Festival's history
- Importance to people who celebrate it

Giving Thanks Web

What is special to you?

When we give thanks, we usually think of what has made us thankful in the past and what makes us happy now. We remember special occasions, like birthdays and other happy times. We also think about the people who have made us happy. On the web below describe the people, events, pets, occasions, objects, etc., that bring you happiness. Also, give a brief reason why they make you happy.

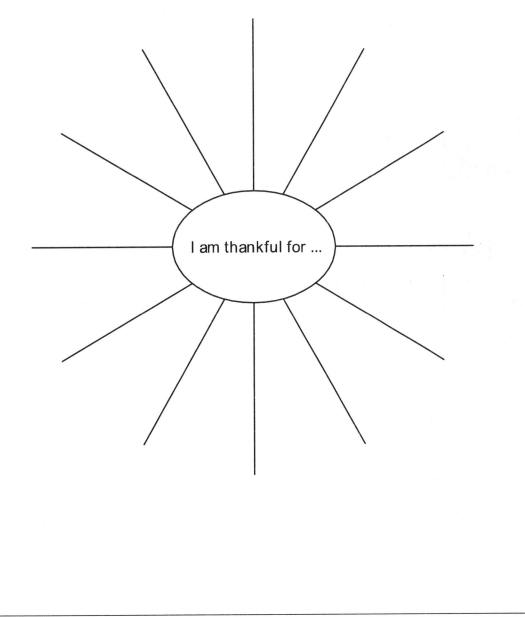

Thanksgiving Puzzle

Complete the following letter blanks using the clues below.

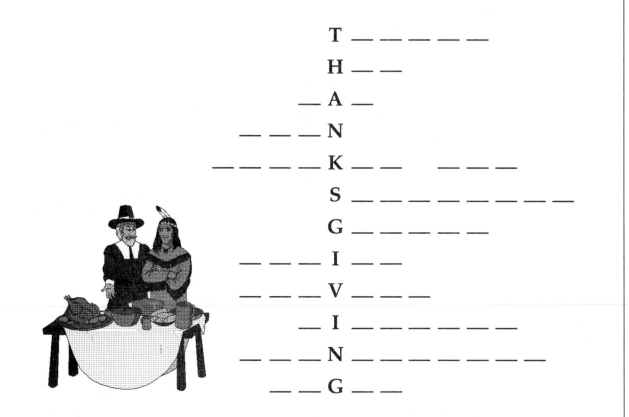

T — — — — —
H — —
— A —
— — — N
— — — — K — —   — — —
S — — — — — — — —
G — — — — —
— — — I — —
— — — V — — —
— I — — — — —
— — — N — — — — —
— — G — —

Clues

T a large, domestic fowl
H dried grass; winter food for animals
A like a sweet potato
N comes on a cob in a husk
K a favorite dessert for Thanksgiving
S a strawman who frightens birds from fields
G wheat, barley and oats are all _____
I Thanksgiving is a time for friends and _____
V we gather crops at _____ time
I early settlers
N red berries, often made into a sauce
G a cart pulled by horses

Hallowe'en

A Night for Spirits

DATE
October 31

NATURE OF HOLIDAY
Traditional

OVERVIEW
This handout provides background information about the origin of Hallowe'en traditions. Many students may be surprised to discover that the holiday began as a New Year celebration. Students may wish to study the early Celts, the festivals of the early Romans, or El Dia de Los Muertos for a social studies report.

Picture Words

As a pre-writing activity have students combine art with words. The letters of the word should become part of the picture. A sample is provided.

A Hallowe'en Comic Strip

This activity master is included for those students who would like to write a Hallowe'en story using a comic strip format. Instructions are given on the page.

Ghostly Tales

As a warm-up activity, have the whole class write a story. Write the first sentence on a sheet of foolscap and pass it to one of your students to write the next. That student then adds one or two sentences and passes it on. This procedure is repeated until all students have had a turn. Photocopy the story or read it to the students. Since the story belongs to everyone, it could be analysed (plot, characters, dialogue, narration, spelling, punctuation, etc.) with the class in an unthreatening manner.

Many students enjoy reading and writing scary stories. Ask them to choose one of the fifteen story starters and develop a plot. As a follow-up activity, invite them to read their stories to the class. Form groups where each group presents a story as a skit, or adopt a Reader's Theatre approach in which the number of students equals the number of parts in the story.

Spooky Hallowe'en Fill-in-the-Blanks

Here is the answer key: Ghosts, Black Cats, Jack o' Lanterns, Owls, Goblin, Witches, Treat, Evil, Skeletons.

Scary Sentences

You could combine this activity with a study of sentence structure. Hallowe'en characters are nouns, their actions and sounds are verbs, and words that describe them can be used as adjectives or changed into adverbs. Brainstorm one or two sentences on the board. Specifically, brainstorm verbs by asking questions: What does a witch do? Encourage students to look up words in the dictionary and to add their own words.

Hallowe'en: *A Night for Spirits*

Many Hallowe'en customs, traditions and superstitions go back more than 2,000 years. The early Celts (pronounced kelts), who lived in the British Isles and France, celebrated their new year on November 1. Starting the night before, Druid priests held a great autumn festival honoring their god of the dead, Samhain. It was believed that Samhain set all the spirits of the dead free on this night; this is where the idea of ghosts, goblins, spirits, and witches first began. To protect themselves the early Celts built large bonfires to drive these spirits away. They also dressed up in scary costumes and masks to disguise themselves, hoping that the goblins would believe them to be fellow spirits and so leave them alone. This is the origin of the tradition of dressing up for Hallowe'en. The black cat, too, is a part of these superstitions. The Druids believed cats were human beings that had been changed into cats as punishment for their evil behavior. Since witches were supposed to be able to change themselves into cats, many people became afraid of cats.

The Romans, who conquered the Celts in A.D. 43, added their own customs to this festival. Apples and nuts were brought to honor their goddess of the orchard, Pomona. Today when we bob for apples we are really continuing an ancient tradition.

When Christianity replaced Druid and Roman religions during the 800s, November 1 was set aside to honor all saints. It was known as All Saints, or All Hallows', Day, and the evening before was All Hallow E'en, meaning *holy evening*. The festivals gradually merged together and the name was shortened to Hallowe'en.

Trick or treat began in the seventeenth century. Poor Irish peasants begged food from the rich. If they were given nothing to eat, they played tricks on the wealthy and blamed the evil spirits.

Scaring Evil Spirits Away

Jack o' lanterns also come to us from the Celtic past. Originally, fierce faces were carved in turnips which were carried as lanterns to light the path and frighten evil spirits. When the Irish, English, and Scottish immigrants came to North America the pumpkin replaced the turnip on Hallowe'en.

In Wales, this night, known as Three-Spirit Night, was a time for fortune telling. In England, it was called Nutcracker Night because fortune-tellers told the future by reading roasted nuts. In Scotland, lighting a bonfire was the custom. As the fire died, each person added a stone to a circle surrounding it; moving a stone would bring bad luck. In Mexico they still celebrate All Saints Day. November 1 is called El Dia de Los Muertos, the day when the spirits of the dead return to visit their families.

Today we may have lost our belief in many of Hallowe'en's superstitions, but the evening is still a time for children to have fun, dress up and go about neighborhoods shouting "Trick or treat."

Picture Words

Choose six of the following words: ghost, pumpkin, goblin, spider, haunted house, broomstick, candy, bat, owl, monster, cemetery, creepy, boo. For each one, write/draw it as a picture word. Here is an example.

A Hallowe'en Comic Strip

Write a story about Hallowe'en in comic strip format. Plan the beginning, middle and end of your story so that it fits into six frames. Be sure to use thought and speech bubbles.

Ghostly Tales

Pick one of the fifteen story starters. Write a ghostly tale of 1–2 pages long. Be sure to include dialogue as well as narration. Illustrate your story.

1. "Trick or Treat!" I opened the door . . .

2. "You're invited to our ghoulish party . . ."

3. A frightening high-pitched sound surrounded me . . .

4. A horrible, eerie ghostly figure drifted towards me and then . . .

5. As I crept up the stairs of that gloomy, dilapidated house, I heard . . .

6. From behind the old, twisted tree sprang a _____ that was . . .

7. I don't remember now who challenged us to stay in Bat Cave that Hallowe'en night, but I will never forget what happened!

8. I noticed the pale face, the crazy eyes, the smirk and the long white teeth dripping blood . . .

9. The night was sharp with cold. The full moon lit our way as we crossed the deserted field.

10. The clock struck midnight. I was alone when suddenly I heard a loud knock at the door . . .

11. The dark-robed monsters mounted the creaking steps, one by one, as the witch cackled . . .

12. The moon, shining through the bare gnarled trees, cast a lonely path on the ground, leading to . . .

13. Thunder roared and lightning flashed across the sky. All of a sudden the lights flickered out!

14. We had dared each other to break into the old, vacant house. Slowly and hesitantly, we set foot inside the door. Suddenly it slammed shut!

15. Witches? Ghosts? They're not real, but . . .

Spooky Hallowe'en Fill-in-the-Blanks

Use the clues below to determine the missing words.

```
            — H — — —
— — — — —   — A — —
— — — —  —  L — — — — — —
        — — L —
        — O — — —
        W — — — — —
      — — E — —
        E — —
— — — — — — N —
```

Clues

H spirits who say "Boo"

A witches' favorite animals

L carved pumpkins

L these creatures hoot at night

O a mischievous, evil spirit or imp

W these women ride broomsticks

E children say "Trick or _____ "

E very bad people are _____

N "bone" people

Scary Sentences

Use words from each group below to make sentences. If you don't know the meaning of a word, look it up in the dictionary. Add other words or change the endings of words (e.g., nervous to nervously) as required.

Example: The gnarled, old wizard cast a magical spell on the ugly toad.

Hallowe'en characters

ghost, goblin, witch, wizard, bat, vampire, jack o' lantern, skeleton, cat, owl, devil, spider, toad, mummy, gnome, gremlin, werewolf

Sounds or actions

pounce, rattle, cast, creep, float, skulk, stagger, soar, fly, transform, swish, boo, creak, hiss, yawn, meow, crash, yell, cackle, hoot, whine, groan, cry, moan, shout, growl, jeer, whisper, clang, roar, snarl

Descriptions and emotions

excited, happy, scared, fearful, nervous, shaken, anxious, terrified, mesmerized, haunted, charmed, ugly, scary, grinning, smirking, creepy, wise, wrinkled, bony, hollow-eyed, gnarled, treacherous, dangerous, magical, shadowy, murky, gloomy, mysterious, misty, rotten, scarred, gruesome, ghastly, horrifying, grisly, hideous, ancient, ghoulish, chilling, nightmarish, malevolent, mischievous, grotesque, frightful

Remembrance Day/ Veterans Day

A Moment of Silence

DATE

November 11

NATURE OF HOLIDAY

Legal

OVERVIEW

After students read about Remembrance Day and Veterans Day, you might ask them to prepare a written social studies report on memorial or peace activities in other countries.

Remembrance Day Vocabulary

You can use this review to check students' comprehension of the overview on the holiday. Here is the answer key: 1. wreath, 2. cenotaph, 3. citizen, 4. custom, 5. ceremony, 6. peace, 7. anthem, 8. war, 9. treaty, 10. veterans, 11. poppy, 12. solemn, 13. memorials, 14. symbol, 15. commemorate.

Remembrance Day Crossword

Answer Key

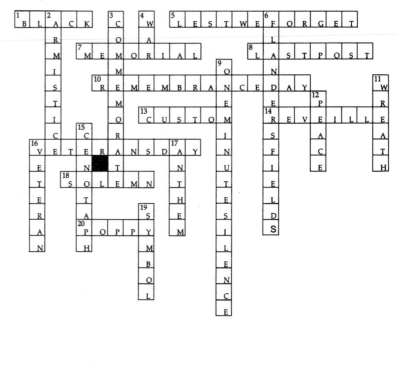

IN FLANDERS FIELDS

In Flanders fields the poppies blow
Between the crosses, row on
row,
That mark our place; and in
the sky
The larks, still bravely
singing, fly
Scarce heard amid the guns
below.

We are the dead. Short days
ago
We lived, felt dawn, saw
sunset glow,
Loved and were loved, and
now we lie,
In Flanders fields.

Take up our quarrel with the
foe:
To you from failing hands we
throw
The torch; be yours to hold it
high.
If ye break faith with us who
die
We shall not sleep, though
poppies grow
In Flanders fields.

John McCrae
(1872–1918)

A Special Poem of Remembrance

Read aloud the moving poem "In Flanders Fields" to initiate discussion about the effects of war on those who are fighting. "In Flanders Fields" effectively shows how soldiers in the First World War felt. It was written by John McCrae, a Canadian army doctor. While he was in Flanders, Belgium, the tragedy of men dying and the sudden appearance of red poppies in the graveyards stirred him to express his feelings through poetry. Linda Granfield's *In Flanders Fields: The Story of the Poem by John McCrae* serves as an excellent resource. It is well illustrated by Janet Wilson.

A cloze exercise is provided to test comprehension. Read the poem aloud slowly as students fill in the blanks on the page. You might want to review the poem's vocabulary first.

Invite students to write a reply (a paragraph, report or poem) to "In Flanders Fields." Have we kept faith? Have we fought for freedom?

Ask students to develop their own webs on the theme of poppies. "Giving Thanks Web" under Thanksgiving provides a model.

Additional Activities

- "In Flanders Fields" focuses on poppies. Students could write a poem about other flowers that are symbols. For example: a red rose, an Easter lily, a provincial or state flower.
- In order to bring the concept of war to a level that students can relate to, prompt the class to brainstorm ways to solve fights or arguments. This could lead to a discussion about bullying at school.

Remembrance Day/Veterans Day
A Moment of Silence

Many countries have special days on which citizens commemorate the sacrifices of those who have fought for peace and freedom. In Canada, the day is called Remembrance Day; in the United States, there are two related days — Veterans Day, also on November 11, and Memorial Day, on the Monday closest to May 30.

On this solemn occasion, citizens honor and show respect for those who have fought for peace. Former soldiers, or veterans, civic leaders, and citizens gather at war memorials and cenotaphs, monuments honoring soldiers who have fought and died and are buried elsewhere, to take part in a public ceremony. Many memorials have the words "Lest We Forget" inscribed on them.

Sacrifices of Soldiers

The playing of the national anthem and speeches about the need for world peace lead into a trumpet solo of "Last Post," a song which symbolizes the end of soldiers' lives. Then there is a minute of silence, followed by the playing on the trumpet of "Reveille," a song of hope. The laying of wreaths at the foot of the memorial is a key part of the service.

The reasons behind the choice of November 11 for Remembrance Day and Veterans Day are interesting. At 11 o'clock on the eleventh day of the eleventh month in 1918, an armistice, or treaty, was signed, thereby ending the First World War (1914–1918). On this date Canadians also honor those who have died during the Second World War (1939–1945), in wars in other countries, and those who have died while helping to keep peace in far-off countries. Americans also remember veterans of the Vietnam War, with some standing vigil by the Vietnam Veterans Memorial in Washington, D.C.

 The poppy, a red wildflower that grows in Belgium where many Canadian soldiers died and were buried during the First World War, has symbolic significance too. Many people show that they are thinking of past sacrifices of soldiers by wearing a poppy on Remembrance Day and the days leading up to it. Symbolic colors are red, representing the poppy and blood, and black, which represents death and respect for the dead.

Whatever your country calls it, this special day is meant to make you stop and think. What will you be thinking about during the minute of silence? Has your life been changed by a war, or the possibility of one? What hopes do you have for yourself and world peace?

Remembrance Day Vocabulary

Match the words below with their definitions:
solemn, commemorate, veterans, memorials, cenotaph, symbol, war, ceremony, wreath, peace, treaty, poppy, custom, anthem, citizen

1. _____ a circular arrangement of flowers

2. _____ a monument to people who are buried elsewhere

3. _____ a person who lives in a city or country

4. _____ a tradition

5. _____ a wedding is an example

6. _____ a state of calm and quiet

7. _____ a national song

8. _____ opposite of peace

9. _____ paper signed by all sides, ending a war

10. _____ people who fought for their country; formerly soldiers

11. _____ red flower symbolizing Remembrance Day

12. _____ serious

13. _____ statues erected in memory of what happened

14. _____ a dove is a _____ of peace

15. _____ showing honor and respect

Remembrance Day/Veterans Day Crossword

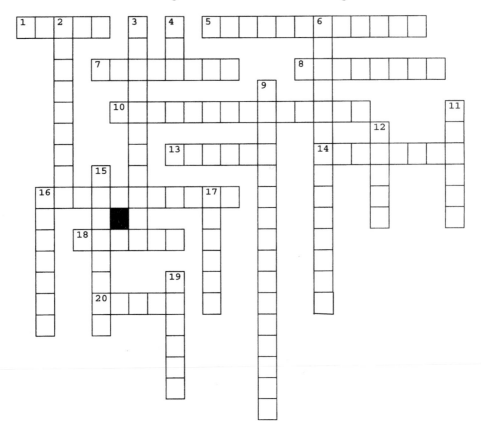

ACROSS

1. opposite of white
5. words written on memorials reminding us to remember those who fought (three words)
7. similar to Veterans Day, but in May: _____ Day
8. a song which symbolizes the end of soldiers' lives (two words)
10. a day in Canada to remember those who fought for peace (two words)
13. something usually done by a group of people to make a day or event special; also a habit
14. the song played after the minute of silence
16. name of this special day in the U.S. (two words)
18. serious
20. a red flower that grew in the fields, where many Canadian soldiers were buried; the symbol of Remembrance Day

DOWN

2. the end of fighting in a war
3. to honor the memory of a person or an event
4. fighting between nations; opposite of peace
6. a Canadian army surgeon wrote a famous poem here during the First World War (two words)
9. a custom of remembering those who died by being quiet for a minute (three words)
11. a large circular arrangement of flowers
12. free from trouble or war; calm
15. a monument to people who are buried elsewhere
16. a soldier who has fought for his country
17. a national song
19. something that represents another thing or idea (black stands for death)

A Special Poem of Remembrance

Cloze exercise: Your teacher will read "In Flanders Fields" to you. See if you can fill in the missing words of this famous poem.

In Flanders Fields

In Flanders _____ the poppies _____

Between the _____, row on _____,

   That mark our _____; and in the _____

   The _____, still bravely _____, fly

Scarce heard amid the _____ below.

We are the _____. Short _____ ago

We lived, felt _____, saw _____ glow,

   Loved and were _____, and now we _____,

   In Flanders fields.

Take up our _____ with the _____:

To you from _____ hands we throw

   The _____; be yours to hold it high.

   If ye break _____ with us who _____

We shall not _____, though _____ grow

   In Flanders fields.

John McCrae (1872–1918)

Eid ul-Fitr

The End of Ramadan

DATE

variable, according to lunar calendar

NATURE OF HOLIDAY

Religious, Islamic

OVERVIEW

The overview identifies Eid ul-Fitr as one of the two major religious holidays celebrated by Muslims. It also provides students with an opportunity to think about people who are less fortunate than themselves.

Eid ul-Fitr Wordsearch

Answer Key

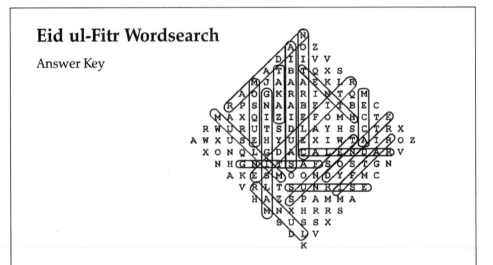

A Day in the Life of a Homeless Person

One of the five pillars of Islam is that people should give to charity to help those less fortunate than themselves. Have the class brainstorm ideas about poverty and homelessness, which occur to a greater or lesser extent in most communities. Ask the students to complete the web for a homeless person. Encourage them to think about such questions as, Who are you? Where are you? Why are you there? What is the weather like? Where are you going to eat/sleep tonight? Who are your friends? What do you own?

Students could then use these ideas to write a day's entry in a journal from the point of view of a homeless person.

Extension activity: Students, working in pairs, could read each other's journals and turn them into newscasts with one partner interviewing the other student who is acting as a homeless person. These could be presented live or videotaped.

Suggest that the class collect food for the local food bank.

Additional Activity

• Invite students to make Eid cards with the words "Eid Mubarak" (Happy Eid) on them. Explain that some Muslims consider it disrespectful to depict people or living creatures in art so advise students to decorate cards with flowers and patterns instead.

Eid ul-Fitr
The End of Ramadan

Eid ul-Fitr is one of the main celebrations in the Islamic year. It takes place on the first day of the tenth month of the lunar calendar and celebrates the end of Ramadan. Ramadan is the time of fasting that continues throughout the ninth month of the lunar calendar. During Ramadan many Muslims get up early and eat before sunrise and do not eat or drink anything again until after the sun has set. By going without food and water during the day people can appreciate what they have in life and gain a better understanding of the needs of others who are less fortunate. Because Muslims use the lunar calendar, Ramadan and Eid ul-Fitr happen at a different time each year.

The exact time of the start of Eid ul-Fitr is determined by the sighting of the new moon. At one time countries started at different times because communication between distant countries was difficult or impossible, but these days when an announcement is made in Saudi Arabia, people all over the world begin their celebrations which may last from one to three days at the same time. Saudi Arabia is important because Islam started there in the seventh century and the sacred places of Islam are in the Saudi Arabian cities of Mecca and Medina.

Remembering the Poor

A duty of every Muslim is to give a portion of income to help the poor and needy. This is called *zakat*. During Ramadan people make donations of food and money so that a meal can be prepared in the mosque each evening. Rich and poor people alike then break their fast with a meal called *iftar*. Prior to Eid ul-Fitr celebrations people give an extra donation of food or money that is distributed to needy people so that no one will be without the means to celebrate the event. This donation is called *Zakat ul-Fitr*.

A few days prior to Eid people decorate their houses, prepare special food, buy new clothes, and send greeting cards to their friends and relatives. During the celebrations people go to the mosque to say prayers. They visit friends and family and join in community activities. People put aside their differences to celebrate this special time together.

A Day in the Life of a Homeless Person

Ramadan is a time for thinking of people less fortunate than ourselves, among them the homeless. Imagine you are a homeless person and complete the following web. Use this information to write a journal for one day of your life.

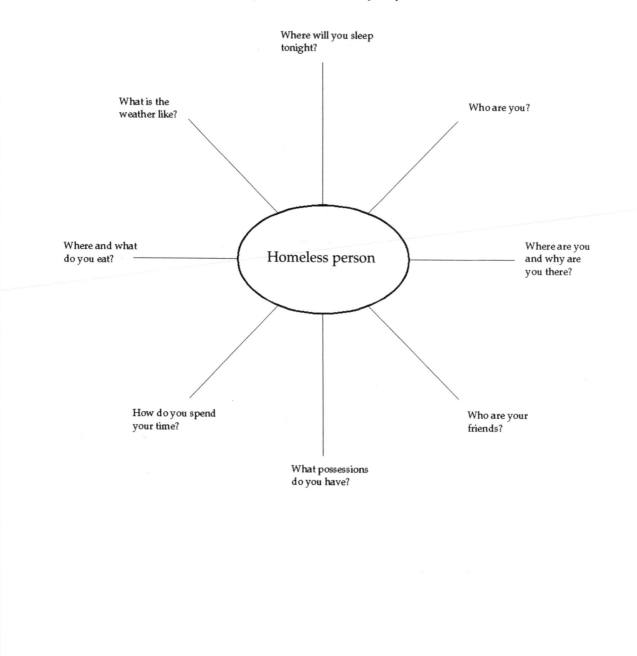

Eid ul-Fitr Wordsearch

```
              N
            A O Z
          D I I V V
        A T B T Q X S
      M J A A A E K L R
    A O G K R R I N T Q M
  R P S N A A B E I T B E C
M A X Q I Z I E F O M H C T E
R W U R U T S D L A Y H S C T R X
A W X U S E H Y U E X I W T A I R O Z
  X O N Q L G D A C A L E N D A R V
  N H G N I T S A F S O S T G N
    A K E S M O O N D Y F M C
      V R L T S U N R I S E
        H A Z S P A M M A
          M N X H R R S
            S U S S X
              D L V
                K
```

Words related to Ramadan and Eid ul-Fitr are hidden in the puzzle above. Circle the words.

Calendar	Celebration
Donate	Eid ul-Fitr
Fasting	Iftar
Islam	Lunar
Mecca	Moon
Mosque	Muslim
Needy	Ramadan
Saudi Arabia	Sighting
Sunrise	Sunset
Tenth	Zakat

Diwali

A Festival of Lights

DATE

Usually in the first half of November; fifteenth day of the Hindu lunar month of Kartika

NATURE OF HOLIDAY

Religious, Hindu

OVERVIEW

Diwali is presented as a celebration of good over evil, light over darkness — a righting of the world. The week-long festival is closely tied to a famous legend called the Ramayana.

Diwali: Festival of Lights Crossword

This puzzle reviews the vocabulary and ideas presented in the overview on Diwali. Allow students to refer to it if they need to.

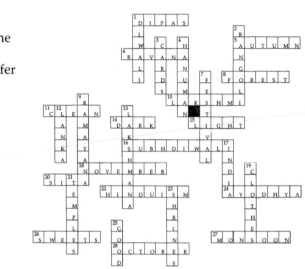

The Story of Rama and Sita

Invite students to rewrite this more detailed version of the legend of Rama and Sita. Encourage them to explore different formats, including comic strip and journal.

Extension activity: Encourage the students to retell the legend as Reader's Theatre. Beyond the basic information in the Introduction, an excellent resource is Mildred Laughlin and Kathy Latrobe's *Readers Theatre for Children*.

Additional Activities

- Invite the students to research a folk story from India, such as the Monkey and the Crocodile or the Hare and the Elephant, and turn it into a picture book. Refer them to *Writing Your Best Picture Book Ever*, by Kathy Stinson, or *Draw & Write Your Own Picture Book*, by Emily Hearn and Mark Thurman.
- Encourage the students to make travel brochures on India based on research at the library and maybe on the Internet. They could combine reports and pictures about cities, temples, history, religion and legends.
- Students may want to explore the Hindu religion by researching gods and goddesses and preparing poster projects.

Diwali: *A Festival of Lights*

Diwali, a festival of lights, is a Hindu festival which originated in India, but is now celebrated all over the world. It celebrates the triumph of good over evil and of light over darkness. Many customs and ceremonies are associated with this joyful time when thousands of little clay lamps, called dipas, burn brightly from every house where the festival is observed.

People want to welcome Lakshmi, the goddess of wealth, to their homes at Diwali, but it is believed that she will not visit any home which is not clean. Prior to Diwali people clean their houses and decorate the floors, especially the floors of doorways and courtyards, with special designs called *rangoli*. Rangoli patterns are often made with colored rice flour, rice or spices. Lights are placed in the doorway to welcome Lakshmi to a house.

Families get together for Diwali the way families gather to celebrate Thanksgiving. People exchange gifts of sweets and send Diwali cards to their friends. They also greet each other with the words "Subh Diwali," which means *Happy Diwali*. They wear new clothes, and those who have quarrelled try to patch up their differences at this time so that they may celebrate Diwali in friendship.

A Time of New Beginnings

People visit temples and shrines to pray. In India people visit the temple at any time of the day to pray, but in other countries there are certain times when people meet to pray together. In India, shrines are often at the roadside, but many Hindu people have special prayer rooms in their homes where they pray. In India, Diwali comes after the heavy monsoon rains have ended so it is the beginning of a new year for farmers. When Diwali celebrations are over, farmers will plant their crops.

During Diwali, plays which tell part of a famous legend called the Ramayana are performed. This story tells of the adventures of a prince called Rama who, at the instigation of his jealous stepmother, was banished to the forest with his wife Sita and his brother Lakshmana for fourteen years. While they were living in the forest, Sita was kidnapped by the ten-headed demon Ravana and taken to the island of Lanka, or Sri Lanka. The monkey king, Hanuman, helped Rama rescue Sita and defeat Ravana. Finally, Rama returned to the city of Ayodhya and took his rightful place as king. Since he returned at night, his subjects lit his way home with thousands of dipas.

Diwali: Festival of Lights Crossword

ACROSS

1. small clay lamps
5. another name for Fall
6. a ten-headed demon
8. where Rama was banished
10. a goddess who blesses houses with wealth and success. She passes by houses that are dirty or dark and so all houses must be lit.
11. like most festivals celebrating beginnings, one must have a _ _ _ _ _ home for Diwali; dirty is its opposite.
14. in most cultures it stands for evil and ignorance; opposite of light
15. stands for goodness and wisdom; opposite of dark
16. written on many Diwali cards; it means "Happy Diwali" (two words)
18. the eleventh month
20. Rama's wife
22. a major religion in India
24. the city where Rama returns to and becomes king
26. favorite foods for Diwali are _ _ _ _ _; some are covered in edible silver or gold
27. wet season
28. the tenth month; Diwali is sometimes during this month.

DOWN

1. a festival of lights
2. colorful patterns which decorate floors
3. what you send to friends and family on special occasions like birthdays, Diwali, and Christmas
4. the monkey king who helped Rama
7. a happy time, when people celebrate
9. a story of a battle between good and evil — Diwali celebrates the end of the legend where the hero, Rama, returns.
12. the island where Sita was held
13. Rama's brother
17. country where Diwali began
19. like most festivals, it is a custom to get new _ _ _ _ _ _ for Diwali
21. buildings where people worship
23. special places to worship, sometimes by the road
25. opposite of evil

The Story of Rama and Sita

Retell the story below in your own words. Feel free to experiment with different formats, such as comic strip, illustrated book, or journal.

Long ago there lived a king called Dashratha who had three wives, Kaushalya, Sumitra and Kaikeyi. Kaikeyi was the king's favorite wife so he promised her two wishes that she could have any time during her life.

When the king grew old, he knew it was time to choose a successor. He chose Kaushalya's son, Rama, to be his successor. When Kaikeyi heard this, she became jealous because she wanted her son, Bharata, to be the next king. She reminded Dashratha of his promise and demanded her two wishes: the first, that Bharata be the next king; the second, that Rama be banished to the forest for fourteen years. The king was very sad when he heard this, but he knew that he could not break his promise. So Bharata became king and Rama was banished.

Rama went to live in the forest with his wife, Sita, and his brother Lakshmana. In time they made friends with the holy men and the animals who lived there and became very happy. Meanwhile, Bharata found out what his mother had done and was angry. He took a pair of Rama's shoes and placed them on the throne. He refused to be king, but said that he would rule the kingdom in Rama's name until Rama could return from the forest.

Whenever Rama went hunting he drew a magic ring on the ground so that Sita would be safe inside it. One day a beautiful golden deer came by and Sita went to stroke it, but in doing so she stepped outside of the magic ring. Immediately the deer turned into the ten-headed demon Ravana. Ravana captured Sita and took her far away to his kingdom in Lanka.

When Rama came home, he discovered that Sita was missing. A little squirrel told him that Ravana had taken Sita away. Rama, very unhappy, searched everywhere but could not find his wife.

Fortunately, Tatayu, the magic bird, was flying over Lanka and saw Sita. Sita asked Tatayu to tell Rama where she was so that he could come and rescue her. Tatayu flew back to Rama. Rama called all the animals together and told them what had happened. All the animals said that they would help Rama rescue Sita. Tatayu would fly overhead to lead the way. At last they reached the seashore, but they were unable to cross the sea to get to the island of Lanka. Then Hanuman, the monkey king, had an idea. He told all the monkeys to collect stones and give them to Rama. Rama wrote the name of God on each stone and threw it into the sea. The stones floated on the sea and made a bridge between India and Lanka.

Rama knew that to rescue Sita he would have to fight the demon Ravana. In a great battle, Rama killed the demon, then he rescued his wife.

By the time Rama, Sita, Lakshmana, and the animals returned to India, Rama's fourteen-year exile was over. People were overjoyed when they heard that Rama had defeated the demon and waited anxiously for him. When Rama reached the kingdom it was night so the people lit tiny lamps to light his way. Bharata was waiting to greet his brother and give him back the throne. Rama became king.

The people felt grateful to Hanuman, the monkey king, and all the monkeys who had helped Rama. To this day, monkeys are regarded as sacred in India.

Every year, people throughout the world celebrate Rama's homecoming and Diwali.

Christmas

A Time for Giving

DATE

December 25

NATURE OF HOLIDAY

Statutory, traditional, Christian

OVERVIEW

The handout outlines many of the traditions associated with this major North American holiday, which is also celebrated in many parts of the world. Discuss with your class family traditions for this special time of year.

Giving to those who are needy is a part of the spirit of Christmas, so many schools organize food drives at this time. You may want to discuss this with students as a way of counteracting the holiday's commercialism.

Students may want to research the Christmas story and the traditions surrounding it. Encourage them to interpret their findings through a retelling or to record the story as a journal entry.

Christmas Time Crossword

Answer Key

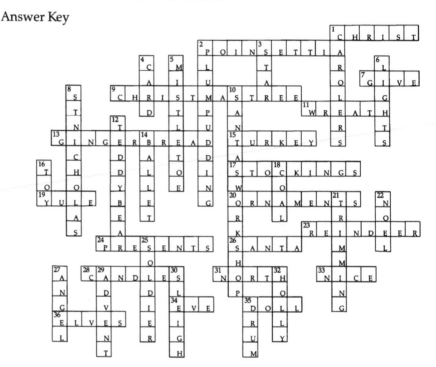

Christmas Cinquain

Instructions for composing this type of poetry and an example are provided on the student activity master. Suggest that students illustrate their poems.

Christmas Tales

Ask students to choose one of the story openers or to create their own to launch their story writing. Encourage them to write rebuses. Explain that a rebus is a sentence in which some nouns are represented by pictures. Create some rebus sentences as a class or have students each create a rebus sentence and exchange it with a partner.

Additional Activity

• Suggest that students write a Christmas or winter song set to a familiar seasonal tune such as "Jingle Bells." Invite them to pick the song first, look at the existing lyrics, and then write their own.

Christmas: *A Time for Giving*

Christmas, like many festivals, began as a combination of the special days of more than one culture or group. It is both a holy day and a holiday. The birth of Jesus Christ is celebrated on what was once a midwinter pagan feast, Saturnalia. Early Christians had worshipped in secret and the actual date of Christ's birth had been lost so in A.D. 325 the Christian Church chose this date, December 25, which is shortly after the winter solstice and the beginning of longer days. Today, Eastern Orthodox churches celebrate Christmas on January 6; in the West this is the date selected to remember the visit of the three magi, or wise men, to the baby Jesus.

The First Christmas

Whatever the actual date, the story is much the same. Since the Roman emperor Caesar Augustus had called for a census, the carpenter Joseph and Mary, his wife, travelled to Bethlehem, Joseph's family home, to register. Because there was no room in the inn, the baby Jesus was born in a stable and laid in a manger. Shepherds in the fields nearby, who had been visited by angels, came to see the baby. And twelve days later according to tradition, three wise men from the East, who had followed a star, arrived and presented Jesus with valuable gifts of gold, frankincense, and myrrh. Thus began our custom of giving gifts.

A Wealth of Traditions

Many Christmas traditions have become established since then. Here are some of them:
- Many Europeans and some North Americans observe Advent, the four weeks leading up to Christmas. One tradition is to have an Advent calendar; each day has a door behind which is a Christmas scene or chocolate. Another tradition is to light Advent candles, beginning on the fourth Sunday before Christmas.
- Boxing Day began as a day when people boxed up their leftover food to give to the poor.
- Christmas candles are a part of both the Greek feast of light and the Swedish St. Lucia celebration when young girls wear a coronet of candles.
- Christmas cards first appeared in the 1840s in England. These were often hand-colored. In America, the first commercial cards appeared in 1875.
- On Christmas Day in North America the tradition is to serve turkey for the main course followed by a rich dessert such as plum pudding. In Europe, the main meal is often served on Christmas Eve and may feature goose, fish or pork.
- Creche or nativity scenes, recreating the birth of Christ, were started by St. Francis of Assisi to teach peasants the story of Christmas.
- Gifts are exchanged at different times throughout this season. In some parts of Europe, gifts are opened on Christmas Eve or, as in much of North America, on Christmas morning.
- Holly is used for Christmas decorations and mistletoe is often hung from above a door. People kiss under the mistletoe.
- Poinsettias, with their mainly red flowers and green leaves, are traditional at Christmas time in North America.

Gifts for Children

- Santa Claus is derived from Saint Nicholas, who lived near Turkey in the fourth century and was the patron saint of children. He gave gifts to children and poor people. In Germany he is called Kris Kringle, or Krist Kindli, the Christ child. In France he is called Père Noel, or Bonhomme Noel. The Dutch brought their tradition of Sinter Klass to North America where the English settlers renamed him Santa Claus. It was an old custom to clean the chimney for the Yuletide and this may be why he comes down the chimney. Today we leave long socks, or stockings, hung from the mantel above a fireplace for Santa Claus to fill with little gifts. (In the past children who had been naughty would find lumps of coal in their stockings.) In Holland people usually set out wooden shoes for him to leave presents in. Santa is thought to live at the North Pole where he spends the year making toys with the help of elves in his workshop. He delivers the toys on Christmas Eve in a sleigh pulled by eight reindeer led by Rudolph, with his red nose.
- The Christmas tree has long been a part of winter festivals in Europe. The tradition of decorating trees comes from Germany. Candles were added to trees to imitate the beauty of stars. Electric lights were first added to Christmas trees in 1895.
- At one time many people could not read, so stories were told by balladeers who travelled from town to town singing the Christmas stories as carols.
- *The Nutcracker* ballet is performed at Christmas time. A young girl dreams her toys come alive. The dance of the Sugar Plum Fairy and the march of the toy soldiers make this ballet popular with children.
- The Twelve Days of Christmas run from December 25 to January 6, the date when the three wise men, or magi, appeared.
- Wreaths have been used since early times to decorate front doors of homes.
- "Yule" is an Old English name for the beginning of the sun's circle (the start of longer days). Christmas, or Christ's mass, is at Yuletide.
- Yulelogs, which represent friendliness and warmth, were first used to honor Thor, the Norse god of thunder. These log shapes are now used for cakes and ice-cream desserts at Christmas.

Christmas Time Crossword

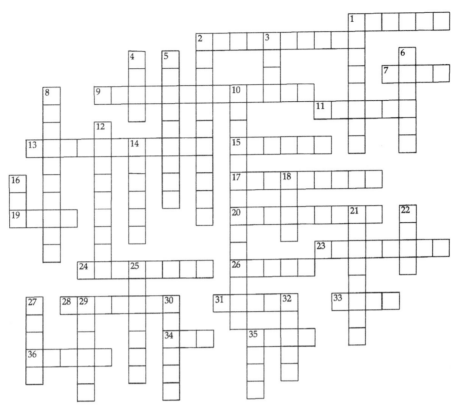

ACROSS
1. the person this day is named for
2. a plant with red flowers and green leaves
7. opposite of receive
9. a tree decorated for Christmas
11. a large circular ornament often made of greenery, flowers, pine cones
13. spicy cookies made with ginger; usually shaped like a little man
15. the bird many North Americans eat at Christmas
17. these are socks that "are hung by the chimney with care"
19. another word for Christmas
20. pretty decorations hung on Christmas trees
23. animals that pull Santa's sleigh
24. items wrapped and placed under Christmas trees
26. a jolly man with a white beard and a red suit
28. lights used on trees before electricity
31. the _ _ _ _ _ Pole: where Santa lives
33. the opposite of naughty
34. December 24 is Christmas _ _ _
35. a toy sometimes given to children
36. Santa's helpers

DOWN
1. people who sing carols
2. a popular Christmas dessert made with dried fruits
3. an ornament hung at the top of many Christmas trees
4. you mail this to your friends at Christmas
5. a branch of this plant is hung in a doorway
6. these brighten up a Christmas tree
8. the old name for Santa Claus
10. the place where Santa builds his toys
12. a soft toy animal
14. _ _ _ _ _ _ dancers perform on the tips of their toes
16. given to some children at Christmas
18. naughty children found this in their stockings
21. when you hang lights, ornaments and garlands you are _ _ _ _ _ _ _ _ your tree
22. French word for Christmas
25. this toy would be found in an army
27. a treetop ornament with wings
29. _ _ _ _ _ _ calendars: each day for four weeks a window is opened
30. Santa rides in this
32. a green plant used to decorate homes at Christmas
35. a noisy band instrument

Christmas Cinquain

A cinquain is a simple five-line poem with one object, event or idea. It uses the following pattern:

Line 1 ---- noun (two syllables)
Line 2 ---- adjectives (four syllables)
Line 3 ---- *ing* words about the noun (six syllables)
Line 4 ---- a descriptive phrase (eight syllables)
Line 5 ---- synonym of line 1 (two syllables)

> Christmas
> joyous, merry
> wishing, waiting, watching
> presents under a sparkling tree
> Noel!

Now it's your turn. Write a poem about Christmas. Use the word Christmas or pick an object or symbol of Christmas or winter (e.g., carols, advent, magi).

Noun: _____

Adjectives: _____

Ing **words:** _____

Phrase: _____

Synonym: _____

When you have finished, write your poem on a separate piece of paper and if you wish, illustrate it with a suitable picture.

Christmas Tales

Write a Christmas story using one of these opening lines or making up your own. Include illustrations or use rebus pictures. The first opening is rewritten as a rebus below.

1. Last year I received the best gift ever. It was not a present or money, not anything you could hold onto. What was it? It was ...
2. Christmas is a time of giving. "Bah, humbug! I just care about the present I'm going to get."
3. When I was younger, I met an old man who told me a wonderful story about ...
4. Two children stood on the sidewalk outside a store window looking at the Christmas tree and presents under it. They wondered ...
5. An angel appeared, or was she just a figment of my imagination?
6. All around the world, children are waiting, watching, hoping ...
7. I was watching TV when I heard a strange noise. Somebody was walking on our roof!
8. "You want a puppy! Who is going to look after it?"
9. What happened to the elves? Where are the reindeer? Someone has kidnapped Santa's helpers!
10. If Christmas is a happy time, then why am I so sad?

Rebus

Last year I received the best gift ever. It was not a  or , not

anything you could hold onto. What was it? It was ...

 Pembroke Publishers

Kwanzaa

An Affirmation of Heritage

DATE

Begins on December 26

NATURE OF HOLIDAY

Recent, North American

OVERVIEW

This festival is all about pride in one's roots. It is not celebrated in Africa, but derives from traditional African harvest celebrations.

You may want to augment the information in the overview with the following details about symbols:

mkeke — a straw mat which represents the foundation of the community. It is on this mat that other symbols are placed for Kwanzaa celebrations.

kinara — a candleholder that holds seven candles. During Kwanzaa one candle is lit for each day. On the first day one candle is lit, on the second day two candles, and so on. The candles represent the seven principles and one principle is discussed each day when a new candle is lit.

muhindi — one ear of corn placed on the mat to represent each child in the family

kikombe cha umoja — the unity cup

zawadi — simple gifts that are exchanged and which represent the rewards of working together

mishumaa saba — the seven candles in the kinara

Map of Africa Crossword

Answer Key

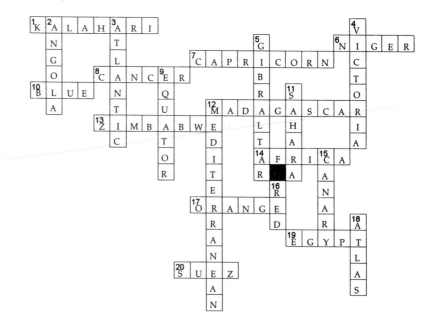

Additional Activities

*   Many people of African ancestry in North America remember their heritage at this time. Kwanzaa emphasizes group co-operation so students could work in groups to research one aspect of Africa which interests them. They could write a story or a report about a topic such as music, an African desert, mountain or river, an animal, etc. Advise students to transfer this information to a poster made to look like a *mkeke*. To make the *makeke* use a beige sheet of manila paper. Draw a border and evenly spaced lines across the paper but within the border. (The lines should go in one direction only.) These lines can then be cut. Cut a separate sheet of manila paper into strips and weave these strips into the large manila sheet. This woven "mat" forms the basis of the poster.
*   Students could research interesting facts about Africa and present the information in the form of a travel poster or brochure. Prior to doing their own research the class could brainstorm what they already know.

karamu — a celebration held on the last day of Kwanzaa and the day when gifts are exchanged

Encourage the students to think about and design a person symbol that represents them.

You may want to read aloud a Kwanzaa story, such as *Imani's Gift at Kwanzaa*, by Denise Burden-Patmon.

You might start the discussion by talking about the equator being thought of as a hot place, but there is snow on the equator on the peaks of Mt. Kilimanjaro and Mt. Kenya and the peaks of the Ruwenzori Mountains. Another interesting detail to mention is that when explorers first went to West Africa they were often surprised to find that villages were expecting their arrival. We now know that messages were sent from village to village by the beating of the talking drums.

- Many animals are found only in Africa, e.g., the mountain gorilla and giraffe. Ask students to research and prepare a write-up on the study of an endangered species such as the lion, elephant, or mountain gorilla.

- The oral tradition of storytelling still flourishes throughout the continent. Students could research an African folk tale such as one of the West African trickster tales of Anansi the Spider. Students could retell their story as an oral presentation, as a drama, as a narration with silent actors or as paperbag puppet theatre. Or, they could look to a published retelling of a story such as Celia Barker Lottridge's *The Name of the Tree* which is based on a Bantu legend, Verna Aardema's *Traveling to Tondo*, or Tololwa Mollel's Masai tale, *The Orphan Boy*.

Kwanzaa
An Affirmation of Heritage

Kwanzaa was developed in the United States in 1966 by Maulana Karenga, a scholar and activist. It has grown more popular throughout the years and is now celebrated in Canada by many Canadians of African ancestry as well. Although not celebrated in Africa, its roots are in African harvest festivals. The language used to name the principles and symbols of Kwanzaa is Swahili, spoken in East Africa. Kwanzaa starts on December 26 and lasts for seven days. It is a time for people of African ancestry in North America to remember their heritage.

The seven principles of Kwanzaa encourage people to work together for their own benefit and the benefit of their communities. These principles are as follows:

umoja — to work for unity to foster and strengthen family and community ties
kujichaglia — self-determination
ujima — to work together to build a strong community
ujamaa — to work together for economic success
nia — to develop individual and community potential
kuumba — to use our hands and minds to make a more beautiful community
imami — to believe in ourselves and our future

Seven candles are put in a candleholder, called a *kinara* in Swahili, and placed on a special mat called a *mkeke*. Each day a candle is lit and people discuss one of the principles and how it can be put into practice to improve their own lives and help other people in the community.

African Inspiration

At Kwanzaa, people look both to the future and to the past.

Africa has a rich history which includes the ancient civilization of Egypt and the kingdoms of Mali, Benin and Ghana. The fifteenth to nineteenth centuries were an unfortunate time due to colonialism and slavery. Africans were forced to work in Europe and North America under harsh conditions. Former American slaves returned and founded the West African country of Liberia in the early years of the nineteenth century.

Africa has some of the world's largest deposits of gold, diamonds and oil, but the resources of wealth are unevenly distributed throughout the continent. Canada and the United States send medical necessities and technical experts to help the poorer nations become more self-sufficient.

African culture and music have had a significant influence on the rhythms of our rock and jazz music. Art from Africa includes bronze jewellery, beadwork, wood carving, especially mask carving, and metal work. Many examples of African art can be seen in museums throughout the world. African communities have a strong tradition of storytelling and many of the stories have spread to other continents. Perhaps the best known character is the trickster found in West African folk tales, Anansi the Spider, about whom many books have been written.

Map of Africa Crossword

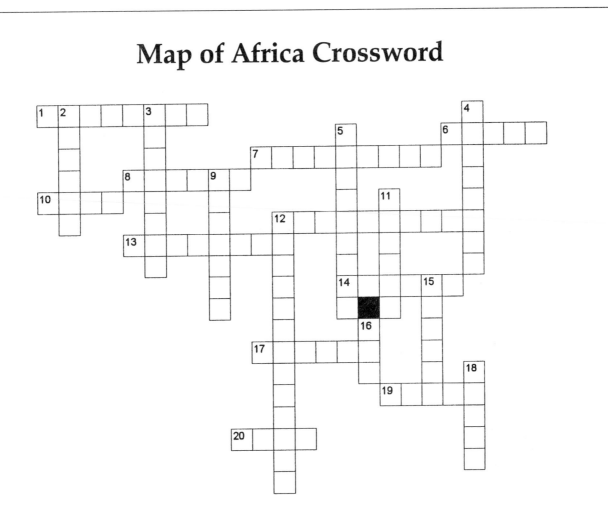

ACROSS

1. a desert in Botswana
6. a river in West Africa
7. tropic south of equator
8. tropic north of equator
10. the _____ Nile has its source in Ethiopia (a color)
12. an island east of Africa
13. country name, begins with "Z"
14. second largest continent
17. river in South Africa; the color of a fruit
19. the last country before the Nile flows into the sea
20. a canal between the Mediterranean and Red Seas

DOWN

2. name of country beginning with "A"
3. an ocean on the west coast of Africa
4. a lake in East Africa; the name of a city in British Columbia
5. a strait between Africa and Europe
9. imaginary line which divides the earth into north and south hemispheres
11. desert north of the equator
12. sea between Africa and Europe
15. islands west of Morocco; the name of a bird
16. the _____ Sea is east of Egypt
18. a mountain range in Morocco; a book of maps

New Year's Day

By the Gregorian Calendar

DATE

January 1

NATURE OF HOLIDAY

Statutory, traditional

OVERVIEW

This handout puts New Year's Day into context and introduces the subject of calendars. Students may have questions about calendars. There are many reference books available on this topic, and there are pages on calendars and seasons in General Celebration Activities near the back of the book.

Thinking about the Good Things

Before handing out this student activity master, remind the students that they can make good things happen. Ask the class to identify positive resolutions they might adopt, for example, getting homework done on time, helping dry the dishes, doing something nice for another person. This student activity master encourages reflection about past and future.

New Year's Puzzle

There are two puzzles on this student activity master. For the contest, ask students to make as many words as they can from the letters of the phrase "Happy New Year"; some are pear, many, any, hear. Remind students that letters can be used in each word only as many times as they appear in the phrase.

Answer key: Happiness, Auld Lang Syne, Peace, Prediction, February, Ring, Eve, Whistles, Year, Calendar, January, Resolutions

New Year Celebrations around the World

"New Year Celebrations around the World" may be used after studying one or more New Year celebrations. (Diwali, previously described, is one.) Let the students complete the organization chart, which could be enlarged, either by interviewing people or doing it as a library project.

Additional Activities

- Ask students, in groups, to take one aspect of a New Year celebration, such as food, and complete a poster. They could also bring in artifacts, for example, red envelopes for Chinese New Year, kites for Korean New Year.
- New Year's Day lends itself to the creation of cinquain poetry, where the first and last lines, each two syllables, mean the same thing. See "Christmas Cinquain," on page 38.

New Year's Day
By the Gregorian Calendar

Celebrating the New Year is a very old tradition. The North American New Year falls on January 1, which is the start of the year in the Gregorian calendar. For us today it is a time of looking back at the old year and a time of looking forward to the new one. Our modern celebration actually goes back to Roman times and the Julian calendar that was named for Julius Caesar. Janus, the Roman god of beginnings and endings, is two-faced, with one face looking back and the other forward. From Janus we get the name of the month January and like him we look back at what we have done and celebrate the possibilities of what we might do in the new year.

The New Year now falls in the middle of winter in the Northern Hemisphere and is a winter holiday. However, it started out as a springtime holiday for marking the rebirth of spring, the return of warm weather and the renewed ability to grow new food. The early Greeks celebrated it in June and the ancient Egyptians in July. In the Middle Ages most European countries still used the Julian calendar and celebrated New Year's Day on March 25. In 1582 the Gregorian calendar was introduced and Roman Catholic countries began to celebrate New Year's Day on January 1. By 1752, this calendar had become standard throughout Western Europe and North America. Today all countries have adopted the Gregorian calendar.

A Time for Partying

In modern times New Year has become an occasion for lively celebrations and the making of personal resolutions, or promises to do something. The holiday we celebrate today has been added to throughout the ages. Our custom of banging pots and pans, ringing bells, beating drums, building bonfires, setting off fireworks and making loud noises first started with celebrations of Hallowe'en. People believed that dead spirits came back on New Year's Eve and so people made as much noise as they could to frighten the evil spirits away. Over the centuries people have added to the party atmosphere so that today it has become a joyous night, a night when we sing "Auld Lang Syne" (written by Robert Burns), count down to midnight and for adults, perhaps toast the New Year with champagne.

Even today New Year is not necessarily celebrated at the same time throughout the world. The Jewish New Year, called Rosh Hashanah, is generally celebrated in September. In China, Korea, Japan, and other areas of the Far East, people follow a lunar calendar to determine holiday dates. In particular, the Chinese celebrate the New Year anywhere between January 21 and February 19. Unlike our North American day, it is their most important holiday.

Thinking about the Good Things

The Year Past	The Year to Come
Good things that happened last year	Good things I hope will happen this year

New Year's Puzzle

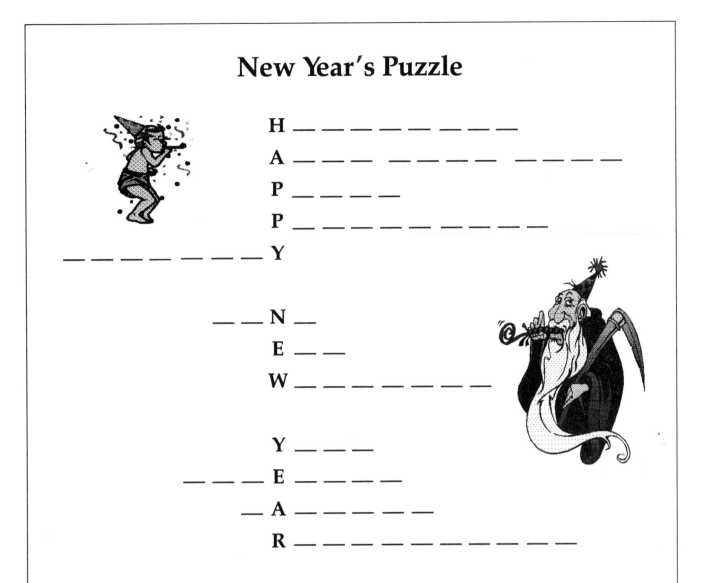

H _ _ _ _ _ _

A _ _ _ _ _ _ _ _ _

P _ _ _ _

P _ _ _ _ _ _ _ _

_ _ _ _ _ _ _ Y

_ _ N _

E _ _

W _ _ _ _ _ _

Y _ _ _

_ _ _ E _ _ _ _

_ A _ _ _ _ _

R _ _ _ _ _ _ _ _

Clues

H What we wish people for the New Year; it is a feeling of joy

A A Scottish song sung at midnight

P What we wish for the world; opposite of war

P A guess as to what might happen in the future

Y Second month of the year

N Bells do this to welcome in the year

E The night before New Year's Day is New Year's ___

W People blow these to make noise at midnight

Y 365 days make this

E This shows us the months and days of the year

A First month of the year

R Promises made for the coming year

Contest

How many new words can you make with the letters of the words *Happy New Year*?

New Year Celebrations around the World

New Year's Day occurs at different times in different places. Use the chart below to show similarities and differences in the festivities in three different countries. One country is done for you to give you a model.

Country	Scotland		
Name of festival	Hogmanay (which is Gaelic for New Year's Eve)		
Date	January 1		
Number of days	one		
History	Long ago people would walk to visit neighbors. The first person to arrive at Hogmanay was called a first footer. Scottish people believed that a dark-haired person brought luck. The first visitor wished the family a happy new year. Today, friends gather at parties to ring out the old year by holding hands and singing "Auld Lang Syne," which means for old time's sake.		
Symbols	first footer — first visitor coal — given to add to fire Father Time — old year newborn — new year		
Preparations	All Christmas decorations are taken down and the house is cleaned. Houses are sometimes decorated with streamers for New Year's Eve.		

Country	Scotland				
Activities/Customs	At midnight people sing "Auld Lang Syne." People wish each other "WaesHael," which is Gaelic (language originally spoken in Scotland) for Good Health. First footers visit houses of family and friends.				
Special foods	Visitors bring bread, cheese buns and sometimes salt. Hosts and visitors drink beer or punch from a wassail bowl.				
People we celebrate with	Friends, neighbors and relatives. Boyfriends visit sweethearts because if they are the first footers and their sweethearts have opened the door to them, they must be kissed.				
Clothes	Usually best clothes, and quite often these are new.				
Gifts	Presents are usually given at Christmas. Gifts for Hogmanay are symbolic, such as coal to add to the warmth of the fire in the house.				
Story/Legend	If the first footer was blond or redheaded it was bad luck. A dark-haired stranger meant good luck so families might arrange to have a dark-haired first visitor come at 12:01.				

Korean New Year

Solar and Lunar

DATE

January 1–3

NATURE OF HOLIDAY

Traditional, Korean

OVERVIEW

This student activity master provides a brief backgrounder to the festivities held at New Year. After reading it, students might prepare a social studies report on the country or a study of its art and culture. One interesting feature is *han-gul*, the Korean alphabet. It was created to replace the Chinese characters which were not phonetically accurate in depicting Korean sounds. Students may enjoy studying *han-gul* and other written languages, for example, Egyptian hieroglyphics. Perhaps there are students in the class who could give a presentation on their own mother tongue.

A Partner Poem

Riding seesaws and swings are traditional activities associated with New Year celebrations in Korea. To emulate such reciprocal movement, encourage students to create partner poems. Working in pairs, the first student writes two lines of the poem and hands it to his/her partner, who then writes the next two lines. Students continue this back-and-forth motion, which mimics the seesaw or swing, until the poem is finished. Subjects for the poems may be decided either by the teacher or by the students.

The Diamante: Opposites

Korean art and poetry feature the heron as a favorite bird. Another common symbol is the tiger. These opposites in characteristics could be used to introduce the diamante form of poetry where two such contrasting images are used in one poem. The Korean flag, called the Taeguk, is also a study in contrasts. In its centre are the ying and yang symbols; the red is the yang and the blue at the bottom is the ying. These two symbols represent the duality in the world: day and night, good and evil, masculine and feminine, hot and cold, plus and minus. The bars reinforce this: the three in the upper left stand for heaven, while the opposite bars represent earth. The lower left bars express fire; their opposite, water. Students may want to write diamante poems using the contrasting symbols of Korea's flag. Instructions are given on the student activity master: winter and summer are used as examples there.

As a prewriting activity, ask students to work in groups to brainstorm opposites. They could write their opposites down and then sort the words into the following categories:

Noun	Preposition	Adjective	Adverb
winter/summer	up/down	strong/weak	slowly/quickly

Additional Activities

- Flying kites is a traditional New Year activity in Korea. The student activity master for kite-shaped poems is found under "Oshogatsu: Japanese New Year" and may also be used here.
- There are many fascinating Korean folk tales, such as those found in *Korea's Favorite Tales and Lyrics*. Students could read one and retell it as Reader's Theatre.

Korean New Year: *Solar and Lunar*

Korean New Year was originally a lunar festival, called Sol-nal, held at the beginning of the second new moon after the winter solstice (December 21 or 22). This means that it would be celebrated at the end of January or the beginning of February. Sol-nal was an agricultural festival signalling the end of the old year and foreshadowing the coming of spring. Nowadays, New Year is officially celebrated on the solar new year, January 1. Sol-nal, or lunar New Year's Day, is now a National Folklore Day, when families honor ancestors, have special food and play traditional games. Both New Year and Sol-nal are holidays in South Korea. For Koreans, these are the most important and joyous festivals of the year!

Before New Year's Day it is a custom to pay all bills. Koreans try to get off to a fresh start. Houses are cleaned and preparations made for the big days. People may go to temples to worship their ancestors or attend church. This festival is not just religious though; it is a time for families and friends to get together.

Everyone enjoys New Year, especially children. They get new clothes, often traditional costumes called *han bok*. As a mark of respect when they meet adults, they perform a *sebae* — a deep bow. Afterwards, the adults give them food, gifts or money. Greeting cards and gifts are exchanged among adults as well. Families eat a special rice soup, called *ttukgook*, for New Year. Dinner might typically include two other favorites, *kimchi*, traditional pickles, and *bulgogi*, thinly sliced strips of spicy grilled beef. In fact, there might be over twenty dishes for dinner.

Much visiting takes place too. In addition to seeing family and friends, adults visit their employers and students, their teachers!

Kites Released in the Wind

New Year is a time for children and adults to play games, including the traditional Yut. Two teams take turns throwing four sticks in the air. Whichever side the sticks land on gets the points. That team then advances around a circle. The winner is the team that first completes the circle. Two other favorite activities are playing on a seesaw and kite flying. Some of the kites have exotic designs and people enjoy kite competitions. At the end of the activities the kites are released in the wind. All bad luck is believed to fly away with the kites when they are set free.

Sol-nal is followed by another festival fifteen days later, when the first full moon of winter, or *porum*, occurs. As part of this festival, called Tae-Bo-Rum, Koreans customarily eat *O-gok-pap*, a five-grain meal. Other special foods are nuts which, according to tradition, give a clear complexion for the coming year. People who live in the country pray for a good harvest at this time. And to conclude the celebrations, firecrackers are set off. Once thought to scare evil creatures away, they are now lit for fun and enjoyment.

A Partner Poem

With a partner decide on a subject for the poem and talk about what you would like to write. Then like a seesaw go back and forth in writing the poem. The first person writes two lines, the second the next two. Continue back and forth until you have finished. Write your good copy on another paper and draw pictures to make your poem come to life. (Hint: Think of opposites such as winter, summer.)

Title _____

By_____ and _____

The Diamante: Opposites

A diamante is a diamond-shaped poem about opposites. It is frequently seven lines in length but can be longer or shorter.

How to write a diamante:

1. one noun
2. two adjectives describing it
3. three *ing* or *ed* words about it
4. four nouns; the first two describing the first line, the last two its opposite
3. three *ing* or *ed* words about the noun in line seven
2. two adjectives describing it
1. a noun that is the opposite of the first line

Seasons

Winter
cold, snowy
skiing, skating, sledding,
icicles, mountains — vacation, beaches
running, playing, picnicking,
warm, sunny
Summer

Now it's your turn.

Title_____

_____

_____   _____

_____   _____   _____

_____   _____   _____   _____

_____   _____   _____

_____   _____

_____

Oshogatsu

Japanese New Year

DATE(S)

January 1–3

NATURE OF HOLIDAY

Traditional, Japanese

OVERVIEW

Invite students to share their ideas and experiences about New Year prior to giving out the overview on Japanese New Year, which may be read independently or as a class activity. As a follow-up you may want to discuss how the Japanese respect and honor all poets. This will lead into the activities.

Kite Poems

Flying a kite is a tradition on New Year's Day in Japan. Invite students to write a poem in the shape of a kite. To prepare for writing poems, students could brainstorm words which they might use, such as kites, the sky, flying, and the wind. Concrete poems are an enjoyable introduction to writing poetry, as the poems have no restrictions other than shape. A sample outline is provided; however, some students may prefer to draw their own outlines, which should be erased so that the words alone form the shape of the poem.

Ask the students this question: From whose point of view are you going to write the poem — that of the flyer, a spectator, or the kite itself?

Haiku

Explain to students that a Haiku is a three-line, seventeen-syllable Japanese poem. The lines are 5, 7, 5 syllables respectively. They do not rhyme. A Haiku usually deals with nature and its seasons, but also frequently includes a person's thoughts and emotions. Explain that a Haiku poem provides an outline onto which the reader can hang an image or may be imagined as a sketch in which the reader fills in the details. Good poems strive for one simplistic meaning or the basic essence of the moment. Examples are given on the student master for Haiku. One technique to provide inspiration is to use pictures of nature in various seasons (from calendars and travel brochures).

Additional Activity

- A knowledge of a culture's proverbs and folk tales is one of the best ways to understand the way the people of that country think. Discuss a couple of Japanese proverbs with the students. Ask them to research a proverb and explain what it means, perhaps using the "Words of Wisdom" student activity master at the back. For a good selection of proverbs, such as "Fallen blossoms do not return to branches; a broken mirror does not again reflect," see "Japanese New Year" under Recommended Resources.

Oshogatsu: *Japanese New Year*

Oshogatsu is an important festival for Japanese people, usually lasting for three days, from January 1 to 3. Some people gather with friends and families to say good-bye to the old year at forgetting parties. They also say hello to the new year. If people have quarrelled, they will try to patch up their disagreements before the new year. Most businesses close, so that people can return to their ancestral homes.

For New Year's Eve, or Omisoka, Japanese dress up in their finest kimonos to go to a shrine or a temple to pray for happiness and health. At midnight, temple bells ring in the New Year. In some places they will have earlier tolled 108 times to rid people of the evil and problems of the old year.

On New Year's Eve people eat a special soup called *toshikoshi soba*. Soba are long noodles which children try to eat without chewing so that they may have a long life. Other special foods are *omochi* (rice cakes), *ozoni* (a soup-stew made of rice cakes), and *osechiryori* (beans, kelp, fish roe).

January 1 is a very happy occasion. Japanese children receive small gifts of money, or *otoshidama*. People exchange New Year's cards, called *nengajo*, which have special red stickers on them. In Japan the letter carriers deliver these cards in the morning, so for them the day is very busy.

Hoping for Happiness

In some areas dancers visit houses on New Year's Day, where they perform a lion dance believed to bring happiness and prosperity to the watchers. In exchange the dancers are given *otoshidama*. People, especially children, enjoy playing games at New Year: for example, kite flying, top spinning, and Hanetsukia, which is similar to badminton. Children also play games with cards, a popular one being Karuta.

Families put up traditional decorations at New Year, many of which are made from pine branches, bamboo, and rope. Pine branches are placed on each side of the front door because they represent the hope for a long, useful life. Straw rope is used as a door decoration due to a legend about the sun goddess, Amaterasu. Amaterasu was teased by her evil brother Susuwano and hid in a cave, making the world dark. The other gods and goddesses tried to coax her out of the cave and when she appeared at the entrance, they quickly pulled her out and blocked the cave by stretching a rope in front of it. That made the world brighter and signified the beginning of a new year.

Kite Poems

Flying a kite is a New Year's tradition in many countries. Think of words that would describe a kite, flying a kite and the feeling you would have while kiting. Then, using the shape of a kite, write your poem.

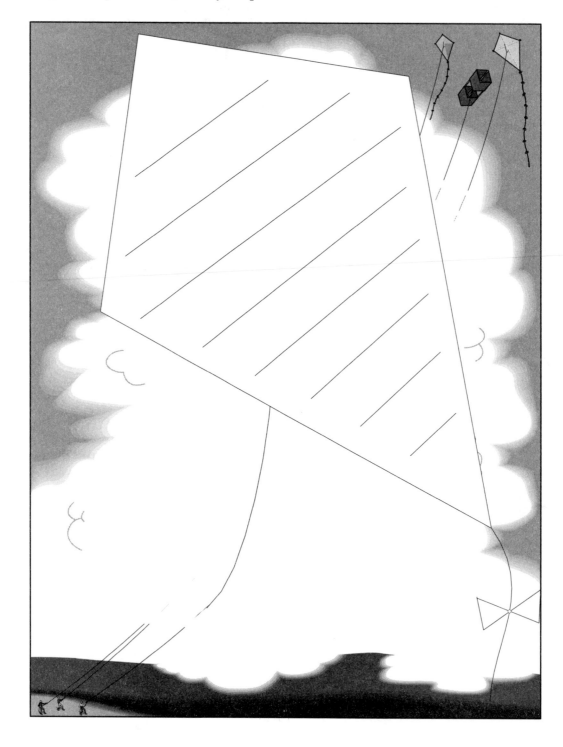

Haiku

Haiku is an old Japanese poetic form. In English versions, it is made up of three unrhyming lines of five, seven and five syllables. Haikus are usually written about nature, but include a thought, mood or feeling about life. Below are two examples.

Helpless

The wild sea rages,
thoughts flee, terror strikes the boat —
a giant's new toy.

Summertime

Lazy summer days,
time out — no rush, no homework,
we stop; we see life.

Now it's your turn. Think of a season, an event or scene that takes place at that time, and a feeling, mood, or idea you have about it. Try drawing a picture about each. Then write a poem using your ideas.

Season	Event or scene	Feeling

Title _____

Line 1 (5 syllables) _____

Line 2 (7 syllables) _____

Line 3 (5 syllables) _____

Chinese New Year

Reign of a Zodiac Animal

DATE(S)

Variable, based on lunar calendar; falls between January 21 and February 19

NATURE OF HOLIDAY

Traditional, Chinese

OVERVIEW

The history and legends of Chinese New Year are outlined in the overview. Invite students to share their ideas and thoughts about the holiday. Ask them what special foods and traditions they have in their families and discuss how these are similar to or different from those that originate in China.

Chinese Zodiac: What's Your Sign?

Ask students to study the Chinese zodiac and write a comparison of their personal characteristics with those of the animal for their year. Discussing both Chinese and Western zodiacs might be a prewriting activity. **Extension activity**: Invite students to draw a family tree, including the animal symbol for the year in which each person was born.

Gung Hay Fat Choy Crossword

Answer Key

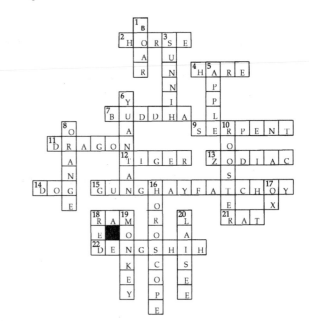

Chinese Zodiac Quiz

This quiz can be used as a test. Answers are as follows: 1. k, 2. h, 3. e, 4. j, 5. f, 6. i, 7. d, 8. a, 9. c, 10. l, 11. b, 12. g.

Additional Activities

- Read aloud a book such as *Chin Chiang and the Dragon's Dance*. Let the groups present the story as skits or Reader's Theatre.
- Ask students to split into groups to research Chinese New Year or the culture of China. For example their projects might be on famous landmarks (Forbidden City, Great Wall, Summer Palace) or art — calligraphy or Chinese painting. Each group will present a report, thereby giving the class an overview of China.

Chinese New Year: *Reign of a Zodiac Animal*

Chinese people use the lunar calendar, which dates back to the time of the first Chinese emperor, Huang-Ti, to mark their festive days. According to this calendar, 1998 is Year 4696 — the Year of the Tiger. The Tiger was one of twelve animals to visit Buddha when he was dying. Each year in a twelve-year cycle is named for one of these twelve animals. The year in which a person is born and its corresponding animal is said to influence or determine behavior in life.

The dates on which Chinese New Year is celebrated vary from year to year. Chinese New Year begins on the first day of the second new moon after the winter solstice, the shortest day of the year — either December 21 or 22. It can be anytime from January 21 to February 19. If you look at a calendar that has the phases of the moon on it, you will be able to determine on what date this most joyous and important of Chinese festivals begins.

Chinese New Year, or Sun Nih, is usually celebrated for five days. In preparation for it, homes are cleaned and firecrackers lit to frighten off evil spirits. Businesses pay all debts to make a fresh start for the new year. People settle old arguments.

Poems wishing health, prosperity, luck and beauty are written on strips of red paper — red symbolizes luck. One common greeting is "Gung Hay Fat Choy," Cantonese for *Best wishes for a prosperous new year*. These poems are hung in the house, especially in doorways and in the kitchen. In rural China, poems are written for the kitchen god, Tsao Kung, whose job is to watch over the lives of the whole family. A week before the end of the year, Tsao Kung goes to heaven to report on the conduct of the family. He is said to return on New Year's Eve. That night a new picture of him is placed above the stove and a huge feast is held.

Striving for Luck

North Americans of Chinese descent enjoy a family feast of nine or eleven dishes on New Year's Eve. Nine and eleven are lucky numbers. Oranges and apples are placed on the table as they are considered lucky fruits. Children are allowed to stay up quite late as it is believed that the longer they do the longer their parents' lives will be.

New Year's Day, Yuan Tan, is a time to exchange gifts. Children give one another lucky fruits and adults give children *laisee*, red envelopes filled with money. Since it is important to have a good start for the new year, children are encouraged to be on their best behavior. Cleaning or sweeping the house is not allowed for three days, as good luck or prosperity might be swept out. Using a sharp knife is discouraged too, as it might cut short good fortune. New clothes and new shoes are worn — old shoes worn at New Year are thought to bring bad luck.

A highlight of Chinese New Year is the famous Lion Dance. Some people in lion costumes dance through the streets, spreading good luck throughout the community. Shopkeepers traditionally hang up lettuce and red packets of lucky money for these lions. If the lion feeds at a shop, it will bring good luck for the new year.

Chinese New Year ends with Deng Shih, the Feast of the Full Moon, otherwise known as the Festival of Lanterns (the full moon is like a lantern). Colorful lanterns decorate the route of this parade led by a huge dragon whose colorful fierce-looking head is made of paper-mache and whose long body is usually made of velvet. About twelve people support the dragon and dance. If you are at a Lion or Dragon Dance parade, you will also notice drums and firecrackers as people joyously welcome in the new year.

Chinese Zodiac: What's Your Sign?

According to legend, Buddha summoned all the animals to visit him before he died. Twelve animals came and each was given a year to control. Chinese believe you will have many of the characteristics of the animal of the year you were born. Find the year you were born. How well does the horoscope describe you? Write a paragraph comparing your personal characteristics with those of the animal of your year.

Rat   2008, 1996, 1984, 1972, 1960, 1948, 1936, 1924, 1912
Rats are hard working and thrifty, but also love to gossip.

Ox   2009, 1997, 1985, 1973, 1961, 1949, 1937, 1925, 1913
Oxen are strong and determined (stubborn). They are artistic — many writers are oxen. Oxen are frequently leaders.

Tiger   2010, 1998, 1986, 1974, 1962, 1950, 1938, 1926, 1914
Tigers are brave and kind, but not trusting. They are wary, just like a cat.

Rabbit   2011, 1999, 1987, 1975, 1963, 1951, 1939, 1927, 1915
Sometimes known as the hare, rabbits are intelligent and calm and like stability.

Dragon   2012, 2000, 1988, 1976, 1964, 1952, 1940, 1928, 1916
Dragons are often politicians. They are show-offs and are loud and proud.

Snake   2013, 2001, 1989, 1977, 1965, 1953, 1941, 1929, 1917
Serpents are successful and wise. They are sharp dressers.

Horse   2014, 2002, 1990, 1978, 1966, 1954, 1942, 1930, 1918
Horses are hard workers, popular and very good to friends. They are also patient.

Sheep   2015, 2003, 1991, 1979, 1967, 1955, 1943, 1931, 1919
Rams are talented, artistic and usually successful.

Monkey   2016, 2004, 1992, 1980, 1968, 1956, 1944, 1932, 1920
Monkeys are funny, playful tricksters who love receiving new gifts.

Rooster   2017, 2005, 1993, 1981, 1969, 1957, 1945, 1933, 1921
Roosters like to be right. They are often dreamy, but seldom angry.

Dog   2018, 2006, 1994, 1982, 1970, 1958, 1946, 1934, 1922
Dogs make loyal, dutiful friends. However, they can be self-centred and stubborn.

Pig   2019, 2007, 1995, 1983, 1971, 1959, 1947, 1935, 1923
Pigs or boars are honest, courageous and proud. They love learning and hate fighting.

Gung Hay Fat Choy Crossword

ACROSS

2. you can ride this fourlegged animal
4. like a rabbit
7. a holy man who had twelve animals visit him when he was dying
9. another word for snake
11. a big fire-breathing lizard
12. a large, powerful, striped cat
13. Western cultures divide the sky into twelve parts to form this; the Chinese base theirs on twelve animals
14. man's best friend
15. Cantonese meaning "Best Wishes for a prosperous New Year" (four words)
18. sheep
21. animal larger than a mouse
22. Feast of the Full Moon (two words, Chinese)

DOWN

1. another name for "pig"
3. Chinese New Year (two words)
5. this fruit symbolizes good luck
6. Chinese name for New Year's Day (two words)
8. a lucky fruit whose name is the same as its color
10. male chicken
16. we may predict our future from reading this
17. a strong animal that often pulls carts or wagons
18. a color of joy and luck
19. like a chimpanzee
20. presents of money given in little red envelopes

Chinese Zodiac Quiz

Match the animal with its characteristics. Write the bracketed letter on the appropriate short line.

____ 1. brave and kind, but not trusting; wary

____ 2. funny, playful tricksters who love new gifts

____ 3. hard working, popular, patient and very good to friends

____ 4. hard working and thrifty, but they also love to gossip

____ 5. honest, courageous and proud; they love learning and hate fighting

____ 6. intelligent and calm; they like stability

____ 7. like to be right, often dreamy, but seldom or never get angry

____ 8. make loyal, dutiful friends, but can be self-centred and stubborn

____ 9. often politicians; show-offs, loud and proud

____ 10. strong, determined (stubborn), and artistic; leaders

____ 11. successful and wise; sharp dressers

____ 12. talented, artistic and usually successful

(a) dog

(b) snake

(c) dragon

(d) rooster

(e) horse

(f) pig

(g) sheep

(h) monkey

(i) rabbit

(j) rat

(k) tiger

(l) ox

Martin Luther King, Jr., Day

Recognizing a Hero

DATE
Third Monday in January

NATURE OF HOLIDAY
Recent, Statutory U.S.

OVERVIEW

Martin Luther King, Jr., is an example of a modern hero who worked to make the world a better place. After reading the overview students could research his life (or that of other heroes).

Martin Luther King, Jr., had a dream for the world. After reading his famous speech you might like to ask students: "What are your dreams for the world? What type of a world would you like to see in the future? What can you do (or what are you going to do) to make the world a better place?" Their answers could be as simple as trying to be nicer, friendlier, neater, etc.

Ask students to write a poem starting with "Imagine a world where ..."

Heroes and Famous People — Are They the Same?

First, brainstorm with students what a hero is. Ask them to name people they think are heroes. Frequently they will confuse heroes with famous people, but the two are not necessarily the same. Heroes have a positive image and are larger than life in some significant way. They are admired and respected because they have done something brave, good or new. Heroes differ from famous people in that they have often sacrificed themselves for their beliefs or causes or other human beings. You might want to point out that our perceptions of heroes often change: Beethoven wrote his *Eroica* to honor Napolean, but after Napolean invaded Russia the musical composer no longer saw him as a hero.

Using Venn diagrams, students could work in groups to clarify their understanding of what a hero is.

Hero Lists

Invite students to create a list of world heroes, legendary heroes and personal heroes. They could include family members as heroes — in fact, mothers and fathers are frequently mentioned and are valid choices. (Some of the activities could be adapted for Mother's Day and Father's Day, especially the certificates.)

Students may share their lists with the class. Discuss the characteristics that help people to become heroes. Point out that many heroes started out as ordinary people. Ask: "Could anyone become a hero?"

Once students have refined their understanding of what a hero is, ask them to work in groups to come up with adjectives that describe heroes. Have a member from each group write these words on the board.

Additional Activity

- Use the words for heroes to create a wordsearch. Some words are heroes, hero worship, heroism, heroine, brave, adventurous, self-sacrificing, superman, and superwoman.

Hero Project

Invite students to choose heroes and research them using the guidelines given on the activity sheet. In order to broaden the topic you may want to allow them to pick famous people, but they should be asked to judge whether their choices are heroes. Students could present their projects to the class using posters, music, videos, etc. As an introduction to their presentations, they could write some basic information on the board: the name of the hero, the hero's country, the hero's lifetime, etc.
Some heroes: Mother Teresa, Terry Fox, Joan of Arc, Nelson Mandela, John Glenn, David Crockett, Mahatma Gandhi, Jonas Salk, Norman Bethune. Lists of world heroes are available in many reference books.

Hero Awards

Modern eros are often awarded prizes or certificates, such as the Nobel Prize or national awards to recognize their achievements. Students could use the generic award format to create a certificate for their hero. They could also do this activity for Mother's or Father's Day. You may want to establish categories and issue certificates to students on an ongoing basis for various achievements obtainable by all students, for example, effort, co-operation, friendliness, greatest improvement.

Martin Luther King, Jr., Day
Recognizing a Hero

In 1983 the United States recognized one of its heroes by creating a holiday in honor of his memory and his contributions to humanity. That man, Martin Luther King, Jr., felt very strongly that people should be treated equally regardless of race, religion or gender. He was also a pacifist, someone who believes in using peaceful means to settle disagreements. An important leader, he inspired others to work towards social equality.

Martin Luther King was born in Atlanta, Georgia, on January 15, 1929. As a young man, he experienced discrimination when he had to attend a different school from his two friends who were white. At that time schools were segregated. However, rather than becoming embittered he followed his father's path and became a Baptist minister. He became active in the civil rights movement in the United States and its non-violent struggle to end discrimination and racism. He was jailed several times for protesting against discrimination and injustice. Even today, people are jailed in some countries for protesting against injustice.

A Dream for Social Justice

Martin Luther King was an eloquent speaker and at a rally in Washington he gave a famous speech in which he said he had a dream that one day people will "not be judged by the color of their skin but by the content of their character."

In 1964 Martin Luther King was awarded the Nobel Peace Prize for his work with the civil rights movement. Although King had initially worked to improve the situation for black people, he had supporters of all races. In later years, he began to fight for people of all races by organizing the Poor People's Campaign. He believed that poor people did not have the same rights and opportunities as better-off citizens.

The Influence of Mahatma Gandhi

Martin Luther King's belief in the effectiveness of non-violent protest was partly influenced by Mahatma Gandhi of India. Both these men had worked successfully and peacefully for social justice, but both met violent deaths by assassination. Martin Luther King was shot on April 4, 1968. He was thirty-nine years old. In 1983 the third Monday in January was designated as a federal holiday in the United States in his honor.

Heroes and Famous People —
Are They the Same?

Write characteristics of a hero and of a famous person in the circles below. List common characteristics in the area where the circles intersect.

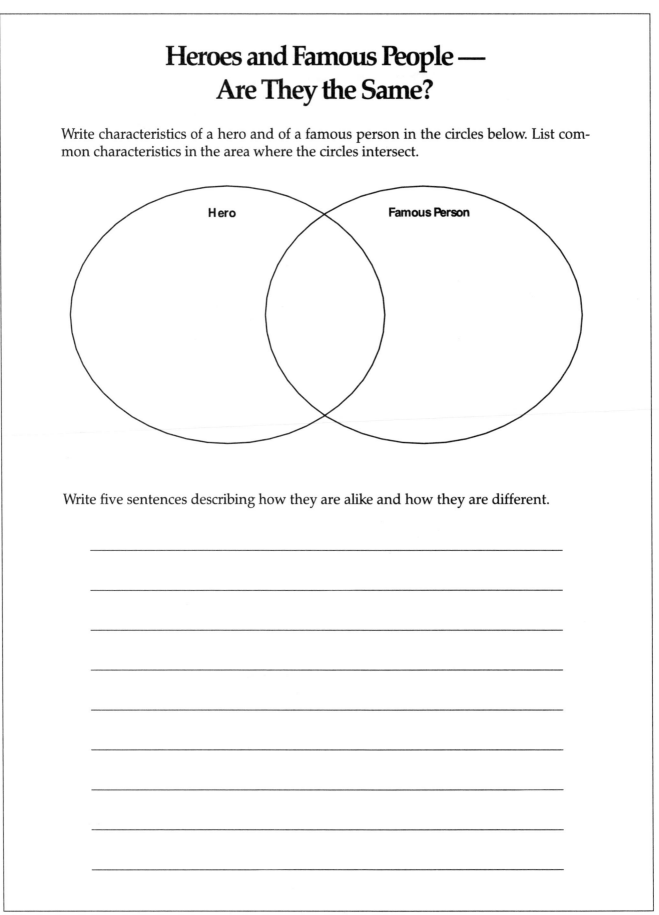

Hero

Famous Person

Write five sentences describing how they are alike and how they are different.

_____

_____

_____

_____

_____

_____

_____

_____

Hero Lists

World Heroes

Hero	Country	Qualities	Contributions to the World

Legendary Heroes

Hero	Story	Qualities	Achievements

Personal Heroes

Hero	Country	Qualities	Contributions to the World

Think about the heroes you have identified. If you could ask them two questions, what would you like to know?

Hero	Questions

Hero Project

My Hero

Picture or drawing of my hero	Background information (country, dates, etc.)

Character traits (three adjectives)	What my hero did that was important

Why I picked this hero _____

_____

_____

What award I would give my hero _____

A poem about my hero . . .

_____

_____

_____

_____

_____

_____

Make a poster about your hero and present it to the class.

Personal Heroes

If you describe someone as a hero, you mean that you greatly admire or respect that person in some way, usually because of a particular quality or skill. The people in your family can also be your heroes or there may be other individuals who are very important to you. Write a paragraph about someone who is important to you and explain why you admire that person.

Design an award certificate for this person with the title "World's Best _____"

Winter Carnival

Le Carnaval d'Hiver

NATURE OF CELEBRATION

Celebrated in Quebec

OVERVIEW

Discuss with the students what a carnival is and how it differs from other parties — it is a season or festival rather than a single event and is frequently held in the winter, particularly before Lent, a Christian period of fasting and penitence. Read the student activity master with the students. It has several words in French which are used in "Winter Carnival Crossword."

The winter carnival is an example of how humans adjust to counteract the severity of winter. Students could research how animals, such as the snowshoe hare, deal with winter. Topics include hibernation, migration and color changes.

Students could research carnivals in other countries or cultures, for example, Mardi Gras, celebrated in New Orleans, Rio, Cologne and Venice, or Caribana, celebrated in Toronto.

Winter Carnival Crossword

Refer students to the student activity master and also make French dictionaries available. The words in the puzzle are in English, but most of the clues are in French. Students may notice several words are similar in French and English.

Extension activity: Discuss words that English has borrowed from French and other languages. For example: esprit de corps, vis-à-vis, joie de vivre.

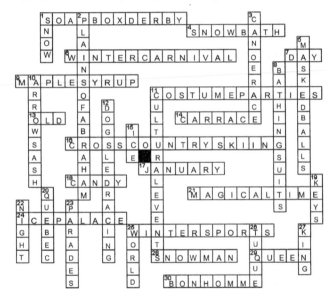

Winter Carnival Sporting Events

This organizer calls upon students to generate adjectives, verbs, and adverbs appropriate to various winter sports. When students write sentences, encourage them to use the verbs, adjectives, and adverbs they have added to the organizer, but also urge them to go beyond it. Students should then pick a sport to write about in detail. It need not be a winter sport.

Additional Activities

- If your school is planning a carnival, invite students to create posters, flyers, cards or brochures to advertise it.
- If you decide to hold a class carnival, have students plan costumes or masks for it. If students know some French, ask them to create posters advertising popular foods in both English and French.

Winter Carnival — Le Carnaval d'Hiver

The Reign of Bonhomme Carnaval

Quebec City, the only North American city to have a wall built around its old centre, is home to the world's largest winter carnival affectionately known by its snowman symbol "Bonhomme Carnaval." The first carnival was held in 1894 to provide a much-needed break for people during the long cold winter. It died out, but in 1955 it was decided to bring it back to life for the enjoyment of those people who call the province of Quebec home and to promote tourism. It has been a huge success!

From the beginning of January to the end of the celebrations, the keys (*clefs*) to the city of Quebec are given to Bonhomme. He reigns as "king" (*roi*) over a wonderful time of dancing in the streets, traditional winter competitions, art exhibitions, colorful parades and funfilled parties. The carnival itself begins at the end of January and lasts for seventeen days. A young lady is crowned (*couronnée*) and becomes Bonhomme's queen for the carnival. People who attend the carnival activities usually wear a "ceinture fléchée," which is an "arrow" sash that is tied around the waist. This is the belt that Bonhomme wears along with a red hat, called a tuque. Another symbol, or *emblème*, is a pin with the picture or figure of Bonhomme on it.

A Magical Wonderland

One of the carnival's most popular art activities is the international snow (*neige*) sculpture contest. Sculptors come to create beautiful designs or statues in hardened snow. Bonhomme's palace used to be made of snow but is now made of ice (*glace*). The Ice Palace, or Place du Palais, takes two months to build and is the largest ice sculpture in the world. It is Bonhomme's home until the end of the carnival. When it is lit with colorful lights at night, it is a magical wonderland. Most activities take place here or nearby on the Plains of Abraham which are turned into a gigantic playground for *sports d'hiver* and *événements culturels*.

The most famous event of the winter carnival is the canoe race (*course en canot*) where teams from around the world attempt to cross the St. Lawrence River. They paddle against strong currents, freezing water and ice. Another chilling event is the snow bath (*bain de neige*) for which participants wear only a bathing suit (*maillot de bain*)! Some of the other interesting activities include a soap box derby (*course de tacot*), cross-country skiing (*ski de fond*), a dogsled race (*course de traineaux à chiens*) and a car race on ice (*le Grand prix auto sur glace*).

For many people the highlights of the festivities are the fireworks and the colorful nighttime parades (*défiles*) that pass through the streets of old Quebec City; for others it may be the costume parties or masked balls. For younger people, their favorite activity might be taking a sleigh or calèche ride or sampling maple syrup (*sirop d'érable*) that has hardened into candy (*bonbon*) in the snow. Night or day, for young or old, winter carnival is a magical time (*temps magique*) for everyone who participates!

Winter Carnival Crossword

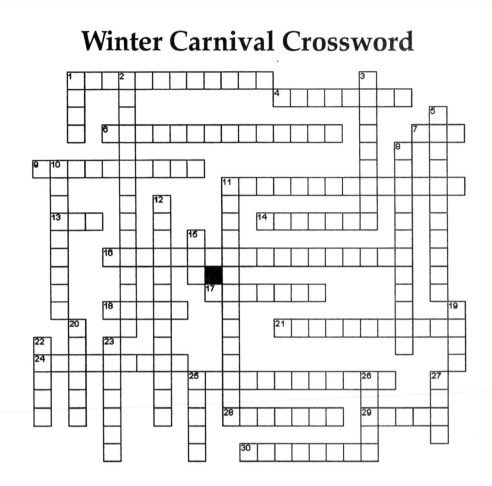

ACROSS

1. course de tacot
4. bain de neige
6. carnival d'hiver
7. jour
9. sirop d'érable
11. réceptions du costume
13. vieux
14. la Grand prix auto
16. ski de fond
17. janvier
18. bonbon
21. temps magique
24. place de palais
25. sports d'hiver
28. any man made of snow
29. reine
30. Carnival snowman

DOWN

1. neige
2. plaines d'Abraham
3. course en canot
5. balles masquées
8. maillots de bain
10. ceinture fléchée
11. événements culturels
12. course de traîneaux à chiens
15. glace
19. clefs
20. name of the carnival city
22. nuit
23. défiles
25. monde
26. Bonhomme's hat
27. roi

Winter Carnival Sporting Events

Cultural events and parties are important parts of the celebration, but for children the winter sporting events and the winter playground are the highlight. Think of sporting activities. What is your favorite? _____

Here are the names of some winter sports. Write adjectives, verbs, and adverbs to describe them.

Sport	Adjectives	Adverbs	Verbs
Soccer	exciting, challenging	quickly	run, kick, bounce
1. Hockey 2. Skating 3. Downhill skiing 4. Cross-country skiing 5. Canoeing 6. Dog sled racing 7. Tobogganing 8. Snowshoeing 9. Snowboarding 10. Snowmobiling			

Use your list to write sentences about the sports. For example: Soccer is an exciting, challenging game because players have to run quickly and kick the ball or bounce it off their heads.

1. _____
2. _____
3. _____
4. _____
5. _____
6. _____
7. _____
8. _____
9. _____
10. _____

Choose one of these three options:
1) Write a paragraph saying why the sport you identified above is your favorite,
2) write a poem about the sport, or
3) tell a story about the funniest thing that happened while you were playing this sport.

Groundhog Day

Anticipation of Spring

DATE
February 2

NATURE OF HOLIDAY
Traditional

OVERVIEW

Invite students to read this handout together or independently.

Subsequent discussions can focus on weather forecasting or on the use of animals in predicting weather, earthquakes, etc.

Extension activities may include studying animals and their senses, or exploring the science of weather forecasting both in the past and today.

Groundhogs and Other Animals

This story organizer provides a structure for students to plan their thoughts about the character(s) in their story and what type of story they want to write. Prior to handing it out, brainstorm with the class animal characteristics (sly as a fox, strong as a bull, stupid as a moose, etc.). These idioms are also similes.

An Animal in Similes

Remind the students what a simile is: the comparison of two essentially different things that are alike in one way. This student activity master provides an enjoyable way to start writing similes. Ask students to combine parts of various different animals, create a name for their animal and write about it.

Animal Idioms

Prompt students to match idioms and their meanings. Ask them to pick one idiom and base a story on it.
Answer key: 1. e, 2. f, 3. g, 4. h, 5. j, 6. i, 7. d, 8. c, 9. b, 10. a.

Also see "Idioms Brought to Life" and "Holiday Idioms" under General Celebration Activities.

Additional Activity

• Review collective nouns for animals, such as flock of birds, pod of whales, herd of cattle, gaggle of geese.

Groundhog Day
Anticipation of Spring

Guess which day is midway between the winter solstice, December 21 or 22, and the spring equinox, March 21 or 22? Yes, you're right, February 2 — Groundhog Day, the day when, as legend has it, the groundhog comes out of its burrow and if it sees its shadow, that is, if it is sunny, it goes back to bed and we will have six more weeks of winter. Well, with winter seeming so long, it's no wonder that people are so concerned about when we can look forward to warmer weather.

This holiday dates back many centuries. The Celts in Britain celebrated a festival on this day hundreds of years ago and like many pagan festivals it was later incorporated into a Christian holiday. Now it is not religious, but rather a lighthearted day when people watch groundhogs to determine when spring will arrive.

German immigrants brought this tradition to North America during the last century. In Germany, they wait for badgers to emerge from hibernation. If badgers are frightened by their shadows, they will return to their holes and winter will last longer. If it is cloudy, they won't be afraid and will stay outside. In North America there aren't any badgers so the animal was changed to the groundhog or woodchuck. The Native peoples of North America also had similar traditions and in many parts of the world people look to animals for signs about the weather.

Making Weather Predictions

How reliable are groundhogs as weather forecasters? What do you think?

Overall weather patterns do help the groundhog and people make predictions. In places such as the east coast of North America, where the winters are generally colder but brighter, there is a 50 percent chance that the groundhog will see its shadow. Winters are usually longer so it is quite likely it will see its shadow and retreat to its burrow. In the western part of North America there is only a 25 percent chance of sun on this day. The northern west coast, actually a temperate rainforest, is usually cloudy and mild at this time of year, so the groundhog is unlikely to see a shadow. Groundhogs and people can usually predict an early end to winter as spring normally occurs earlier there.

Today satellite information gives us more reliable forecasts about the weather, but they are not as much fun as this furry little animal and the superstition that surrounds it.

Groundhogs and Other Animals

Groundhog Day is a good example of animal folklore. Stories about animals are not only interesting to read, but also fun to write. Choose an animal you would like to write about. Research its habits, characteristics and opinions people have about it (for example, a fox is clever, sly or cunning). Write a short tale about your animal. You may also like to include a person or another animal in your story. These guidelines will help you get started.

Animal: _____   **Its story name**: _____

Where I can find it: _____

Physical description	Words that describe it
_____	_____
_____	_____
_____	_____
_____	_____
_____	_____
_____	_____

Type of story (action, adventure, love, family): _____

My idea (plot, storyline) **in one sentence**: _____

Rough copy of my story: _____

_____

_____

_____

_____

_____

_____

_____

_____

_____

An Animal in Similes

Make your own silly, mixed-up animal by combining different parts of other animals. Draw a picture of it, give it a name, then write a poem about it using similes. A simile is a figure of speech that compares two unlike things and is often introduced by "like" or "as."

Name of Animal	Title of Poem

Picture	Poem

Animal Idioms

Match the definition on the right with the idiom on the left.

   ____ 1. A wild goose chase   a) A person may not be what they seem

   ____ 2. Bark up the wrong tree   b) Being very careful with what you say or do

   ____ 3. Birds of a feather flock together   c) First-hand knowledge

   ____ 4. Crocodile tears   d) Someone bothers you

   ____ 5. Dog tired   e) A waste of time or unnecessary chase

   ____ 6. Eat like a horse   f) Getting the wrong idea

   ____ 7. Ruffle your feathers   g) People with the same attitudes tend to be

   ____ 8. Straight from the horse's mouth   friends

   ____ 9. Walking on egg shells   h) Fake tears

   ____ 10. Wolf in sheep's clothing   i) Eat a lot

                                           j) Very tired

Pick one idiom and write a story that explains the idiom through action. Be sure to use the idiom in your story. You might also want to illustrate it.

St. Valentine's Day

A Time to Show Love

DATE

February 14

NATURE OF HOLIDAY

Traditional

OVERVIEW

This student activity master on St. Valentine's Day may be used to initiate a discussion about the holiday and its symbolism.

You could give each student a piece of red 8" x 11" manila tag on which you have previously outlined a heart. Have students write their names on the back, cut out the heart and decorate. They then pass their hearts around the room for others to write Valentine's greetings addressed to them. As a warm-up activity, you might want to lead a discussion about what is suitable to write.

St. Valentine's Day Crossword

After reading the overview, students may enjoy completing this puzzle.

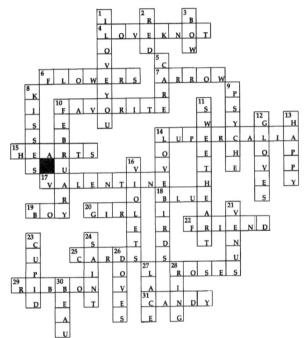

This I Love

St. Valentine's Day can be turned into a celebration of more than interpersonal relationships by looking at what we love. As a prewriting activity, work through one student activity master with the class as a whole and then ask students to complete their own sheets. Let students take a blank page and create a composite picture, with the subject, perhaps a pet cat, as focus. Conclude by having them weave their images into a poem or story.

Additional Activities

- Invite students to research the story of St. Valentine and retell it as a comic strip. See "Hallowe'en" for the format.
- Ask students to draw sociograms of the important people in their lives. They should place themselves in the centre and identify the key people around them. Arrows indicate the direction of the relationship: double arrows, if it is reciprocal; a single arrow, if it is one-sided. On the arrows, they write the nature of the relationship, for example, loving.

St. Valentine's Day
A Time to Show Love

It's a time for fun, hearts, roses, chocolates and special friends.

Who St. Valentine was is a big mystery! There were actually two Christian martyrs; both were called Valentine and both were executed on February 14. In one story a young priest, Valentinus, had been thrown in jail and was beheaded on February 14, A.D. 270. Legend says through his faith he had restored the eyesight of his jailer's daughter. Supposedly he sent her a letter the night before he died and signed it — *from your Valentine.*

St. Valentine's Day was originally called the Feast of Lupercalia, a Roman festival for young lovers. Although Lupercalia was held on February 15, at some point it was moved up by a day and St. Valentine became the protecting saint of all friends and lovers.

Hearts and Flowers

Here are a few facts to share with your friends.

- The oldest known romantic Valentine card was sent from jail. In 1415, Charles, Duke of Orleans, sent a love note to his wife while he was imprisoned in the Tower of London. During Victorian times cards were often trimmed with lace to make them special. Much later anonymous cards became very popular. Many people believed that it was bad luck to sign your card, that you would never marry your Valentine if you did this. Today there are approximately 150 million cards sent in North America for St. Valentine's Day.
- Next to roses, chocolates are the most popular gifts to send to people on St. Valentine's Day. Of course, they should be sent in heart-shaped boxes!
- In North America the flower of love is the red rose. In Denmark, it is the snowdrop. In medieval times it was the violet.
- Long ago people believed that the heart was the source of our feelings. It is still a symbol of love today. Today almost everything associated with St. Valentine's Day features hearts: balloons, teddy bears with red hearts, mugs, pictures, etc.
- Lovebirds always look as if they are kissing and doves are a symbol of love and peace. Both birds are commonly used on St. Valentine's cards.
- During Lupercalia, boys drew the names of girls by lot and courted them the following year.
- St. Valentine's Day has always been a popular time to become engaged. An engagement ring is often given to a woman by her boyfriend, or beau (who then becomes her fiancé).
- The colloquial expression "tie the knot" is used to describe getting married. The two ropes would then be one and have no end or beginning, forming a love-knot.
- Venus is the Roman goddess of beauty; Cupid, her son, with his bow and arrow, is the god of love. Supposedly if you were hit by one of his arrows which had been dipped in a love potion you would fall in love with the next person you saw. Ironically, Cupid accidentally hit himself with an arrow and fell in love with a beautiful young mortal named Psyche.

St. Valentine's Day Crossword

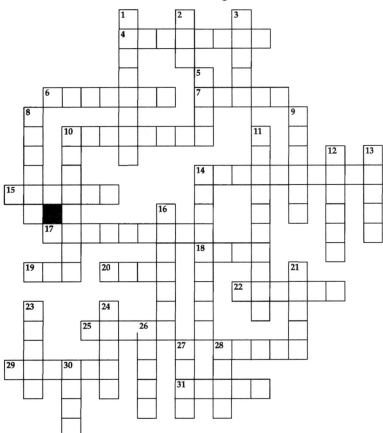

ACROSS

4. winding and interlacing loops with no beginning or end: a symbol of love
6. blossoms
7. Cupid shoots this to make you fall in love
10. what you like best
14. an ancient festival that St. Valentine's Day is based on
15. symbols of love
17. the person this day is named for
18. the color of sadness
19. opposite of girl
20. opposite of boy
22. a person you like and can trust
25. greetings are sent to people on these
28. a favorite flower for St. Valentine's Day
29. a long narrow piece of material used for tying things
31. a sweet confection

DOWN

1. what you say to someone you love (three words)
2. the color for this day
3. used to shoot arrows with
5. to feel friendship or love for another person
8. touches with lips in order to show affection
9. a beautiful mortal beloved by Cupid
10. the second month of the year
11. a term used to describe the person you love
12. coverings for your hands; in olden times a man would give these to ask for a woman's hand in marriage
13. opposite of sad
14. colorful parrots who sit very closely together as if kissing
16. flowers of love in medieval times
21. goddess of love
23. god of love (a little boy with a bow and arrow)
24. what Valentine was
26. birds that are symbols of love and peace
27. pretty cloth with holes in it made from fine thread and often used around Valentine's cards
28. what you give to someone when you get engaged or married
30. French word meaning boyfriend

This I Love

What are the things you love or like a lot? Under each heart write the word(s) and in the hearts create pictures that illustrate the word(s). For example, if your favorite color is grey, your picture must be of something that is grey, e.g., pussywillows, whales, rocks.

Color: _____

Texture: _____

Sound: _____

Subject: _____

Mood words: _____

Smell/aroma: _____

Scene: _____

On plain paper create a large drawing beginning with the subject you have identified and adding all the other things you love into the picture. When it is finished, color it and then write a poem or story about your picture.

St. Patrick's Day

Wearing the Green

DATE
March 17

NATURE OF HOLIDAY
Traditional

OVERVIEW

Students will gain a brief history of this colorful day. There are many possible follow-up activities.

You could invite students to research folk tales about St. Patrick. Students could then create a bio-sketch or skit about him. Or, working in pairs, one student could role-play St. Patrick while another conducts an interview.

Ask students to write a story in which St. Patrick time-travels to another century. What do they think he would feel about the day that honors him?

As a class, have students brainstorm the many ways the words spring and green are used. Later, encourage them to organize the words into a shape poem of something green, for example, a shamrock, tree or leaf. Ask them to sketch the shape in pencil first, then, after the words of the poem have filled the shape, to erase the outer edges.

You can use "Symbols," "Idioms Brought to Life," and "Holiday Idioms" from General Celebration Activities here.

St. Patrick's Day Crossword

See the answer key below. Alternatively, ask students, in pairs, to develop their own crossword puzzles and answers and to exchange puzzles with another pair of students for completion.

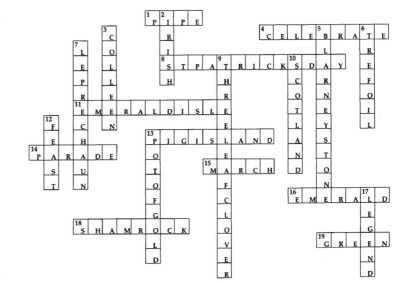

Pot of Words

This puzzle is designed to stimulate vocabulary development and to provide fun. Encourage students to consult their dictionaries if they're not sure something is a real word. In our experience, students find between fifty and 200 words.

St. Patrick and the Slithery Snakes

Students are usually fascinated by the tale of St. Patrick driving out the snakes from Ireland. This organizer provides several topics to pursue from science reports to story or poetry writing.

Limericks

Many St. Patrick's Day stories are exaggerations and so the holiday is an excellent time to teach students how to write a limerick. The student activity master explains what a limerick is and how to write it. You might invite the whole class to write a limerick together before students compose their own. Mention that limericks should not poke fun at others in the class.

St. Patrick's Day: *Wearing the Green*

On March 17 many people, even those who are not of Irish descent, wear something green to honor St. Patrick, the patron saint of Ireland, who lived from about A.D. 387 to 461.

The legends about St. Patrick paint a colorful picture of this man. It is believed that he was born in either Scotland or Wales, but was captured by pirates when he was sixteen and taken to Ireland where he was sold into slavery. He later escaped, fled to France and studied for many years at a monastery. Eventually he became a bishop and returned to Ireland to Christianize the Celtic people. Once there he preached, taught, built churches, organized schools and performed miracles.

There are many tales about the miracles he performed. He turned snow and ice into fire and a wolf dog into stone. What he is most famous for is driving all of the snakes out of Ireland. Strangely enough, Ireland has *no* snakes!

Adopting the Shamrock

Old ideas are often included in new rituals. The Druids of Ireland used the shamrock as a symbol in their religion. According to legend, St. Patrick took the shamrock, which is a three-leaf clover (a trefoil) and used it as a religious symbol. Today the shamrock is the national flower of the Republic of Ireland and the symbol for St. Patrick's Day.

Here are some other fascinating facts about the day:
- Green is the color of Ireland, nicknamed the Emerald Isle. Long ago Ireland was called Pig Island because many people there raised pigs.
- Green is the color used to dye many items for St. Patrick's Day, including green cookies, cakes and milkshakes.
- Leprechauns are small, roguish elves. They are known for their bad tempers and pots of gold, which are supposedly at the ends of rainbows. If you keep a leprechaun in sight, he will be forced to take you to his money.
- Many of the people celebrating this day are not of Irish descent, but enjoy the fun and frivolity it brings.
- March 17 is the day St. Patrick died, not the day he was born.
- The blarney stone is a stone that is supposed to possess special powers. Kiss it and you'll have the gift of sweet talk and flattery. Many visitors to Ireland do kiss it!
- The nickname for any young Irish girl is a colleen.
- The top hat, cane and short pants with white socks seen in many pictures are the old-fashioned clothes of the Irish countryman.
- This day is often thought of as the beginning of spring.
- Wearing o' the green probably began as a substitute to wearing shamrock leaves. Shamrocks are not common in North America so people wore something green instead!

St. Patrick's Day Crossword

ACROSS

1. used to smoke tobacco
4. what you do at parties
8. March 17 is his day (three words)
11. nickname for Ireland (two words)
13. an ancient name for Ireland; boars are often in Irish legends (two words)
14. a special event or progression held on the streets of a city
15. St. Patrick's Day is in this month
16. a precious green gem
18. a three-leaf clover
19. the color of Ireland

DOWN

2. name for the people of Ireland
3. nickname for any Irish girl
5. a special stone; kiss it and you will have the gift of sweet talk and flattery (two words)
6. another name for the shamrock
7. a small, roguish elf
9. what a shamrock is (three words)
10. country where St. Patrick was thought to be born
12. a big dinner
13. this is said to be at the end of a rainbow (three words)
17. a story about people such as St. Patrick

Pot of Words

Fill the leprechaun's pot with words made up from the letters of the word *Leprechaun.*

St. Patrick and the Slithery Snakes

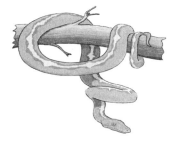

A fascinating legend about St. Patrick relates to how he drove the snakes out of Ireland. Research the legend in the library. Pick one of the following three topics about St. Patrick or snakes to present to your class.

Present the legend to your class. You may choose to rewrite it as a comic strip; present it as an illustrated poster; or work with a small group to write a script and act it out for the class.

Research a snake which you find fascinating and present a detailed report to the class. Include pictures and unusual facts.

Compose a snake poem or story. Write all of the words that you can think of to describe snakes. For example, snakes are sudden, slithery ...

This organizer will help you think about snakes.

Appearance	Actions

Descriptive Words	How I Feel about Them

Use as many of these words as you can in writing your snake poem, story or report. If you are writing a poem, you might like to write it in the shape of a snake.

Limericks

Limericks have been a popular form of humor for hundreds of years. They are sometimes nonsensical and often poke fun at people's actions, habits and idiosyncrasies.

The five lines of a limerick must follow a set pattern:
• The first line identifies the person, perhaps saying where he/she is from.
• The second line mentions one strange feature.
• Lines 3 and 4 develop the picture about this strange habit.
• The final line offers a funny or unique twist to what has already been said about the person.

Because limericks are meant to be oral, the rhythm in each line is important. Lines one, two and five should have three accented beats contrasted with lines three and four which have two accented beats. In addition, a limerick must have a rhyme scheme; a popular one is *aabba*.

There once was a man from Killarney
Who had the rare gift of the Blarney
    He chatted all night
    His face, it turned white
That talkative man from Killarney!

Now it's your turn!

There once was a _____ named (or from) _____

Who_____

_____

_____

_____

Passover

From Slavery to Freedom

DATES

Usually in late March/early April; based on the lunar Hebrew calendar

NATURE OF HOLIDAY

Religious — Jewish

OVERVIEW

The handout provides a brief summary of the story of Passover and the foods eaten for Seder, on the first and second nights of Passover. Should you wish to have the class know more about the religious aspects there are many books available. *The Passover Journey*, by Barbara Goldin, is well written, very comprehensive and age-appropriate.

Passover Wordsearch

Answer Key
Note: Individually circled letters are used in two different words.

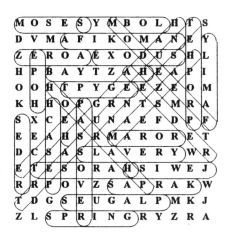

Passover Research

Passover involves learning about the history of the story as well as the Seder ceremony. As such, we feel that it should be studied from a social studies perspective first, followed by language arts activities. We suggest dividing the class into groups and encouraging students to pick topics of interest to them. Since some activities are more challenging than others, assist students in picking activities suitable to their abilities. For Group 4, you should be able to suggest a few resource persons. If possible, arrange for someone to speak to the whole class.

In discussing Passover as a story of slaves striving to be free, you could ask students if they are aware of other groups who have faced similar problems. (Americans of African descent would be one example.)

Passover: *From Slavery to Freedom*

One of the most important holidays to Jewish families is Passover, or Pesach (Hebrew for "passing over"), which begins in March or April and lasts for seven or eight days. Passover celebrates the exodus of the Hebrews from slavery in ancient Egypt more than 3,000 years ago. Although customs vary, all Jews follow the instructions, stories, songs and prayers of the *Haggadah*, an ancient book that explains the Passover story.

The pharaohs, or kings of Egypt, had enslaved the Hebrews, or Israelites, for many years. In the thirteenth century B.C., Moses, the leader of the Hebrews, asked the pharaoh to free his people. When the pharaoh refused, Moses told him that God would send plagues to Egypt if he didn't change his mind. The pharaoh didn't believe Moses and ten plagues were sent: water turned to blood; frogs covered the land; dust turned to lice and insects filled the air; wild beasts attacked and frightened the Egyptians; cattle, horses, and camels became diseased and died; Egyptians broke out in sores and boils; fiery hail fell from the sky; locusts swarmed and destroyed crops; darkness occurred in the middle of the day; all firstborn children and animals died.

Before the last plague, Moses warned the Hebrews to mark their doors with the blood of a paschal (sacrificed) lamb, so that their house would be "passed over" by the Angel of Death. This is how Passover got its name.

After the last plague the pharaoh agreed to let the Hebrews go. When the Hebrews came to the Red Sea, they were caught between the sea and the pharaoh's soldiers, who were following them because the pharaoh had changed his mind. Suddenly a miracle occurred: the sea parted and they escaped. When the Egyptian soldiers tried to follow, the waters closed over them. The Hebrews were free at last.

The Significance of the Seder

On the first two nights of Passover families have a symbolic feast called the Seder when the Passover story is retold. In the centre of the dinner table is the Seder plate containing special foods. Each of these foods symbolizes some part of the ordeal the Hebrews experienced: Zeroa, a roasted lamb bone, and Baytzah, a roasted egg — reminders of the sacrifices made to God; Maror, bitter herbs — horseradish and romaine lettuce — reminders of the bitterness of slavery; Haroset, an apple and nut mixture — symbols of the mortar used while the Hebrews were forced to build for the pharaoh; and Karpas, parsley, lettuce, or celery — symbols of springtime and rebirth. Near the Seder plate there will be three matzot (plural for matzah), flat, unleavened bread indicating how quickly the Hebrews had had to leave Egypt; a bowl of salt water, symbolic of the tears of the slaves; wine and wine cups, with a large beautiful cup for the prophet Elijah. The dining room door is left open for Elijah to come through.

During the Seder dinner the family follows the fourteen steps given in the *Haggadah*. The dinner involves both the oldest and the youngest members of the family. In one part of the telling of the Passover story young children ask four questions about this holiday and a family member reads the answers from the *Haggadah*. A highlight of the dinner for young children is the Afikoman when they have a treasure hunt searching for a piece of matzah and a small prize. The ceremony ends with the singing of traditional songs.

The Passover story not only reminds Jewish people of what their ancestors went through in order to achieve their freedom, but inspires all people who value freedom, hope and peace.

Passover Wordsearch

```
M O S E S Y M B O L H T S
D V M A F I K O M A N E Y
Z E R O A E X O D U S H L
H P B A Y T Z A H E A P I
O O H T P Y G E E Z E O M
K H H O P G R N T S M R A
S X C E A U N A E F D P F
E E A H S R M A R O R E T
D C S A S L A V E R Y W R
E T E S O R A H S I W E J
R R P O V Z S A P R A K W
T D G S E U G A L P M K J
Z L S P R I N G R Y Z R A
```

Words related to Passover are hidden in the puzzle above. Circle the words.

Pharaoh	Jewish	Maror
Afikoman	Prophet	Moses
Egypt	Seder	Passover
Family	Spring	Pesach
Haggadah	Treasure Hunt	Plagues
Hope	Baytzah	Red Sea
Karpas	Exodus	Slavery
Matzah	Freedom	Symbol
Peace	Haroset	Zeroa

Passover Research

Become more familiar with Passover by completing a class project on the festival. After discussing Passover with your teacher and the class, join one of the following groups. As a group, research your topic using library resources, the Internet and interviews, as appropriate. Discuss with your teacher how to present your information and share it with the class.

Group 1: Research the story of Passover, making sure to refer to the overview. Present the story, or a part of it, by retelling, using Reader's Theatre, or writing the event as a newspaper story (pretend you are a reporter living at that time and be sure to answer the 5Ws — who, what, where, when, why).

Group 2: Research the Seder, describing the foods and traditions. Perhaps you could prepare a Seder plate. Include the fourteen steps and the four questions as part of your project.

Group 3: Research current-day Egypt, Israel, or neighboring countries. Present your findings in the form of a newscast or as a newspaper page.

Group 4: As a group, discuss what makes a successful interview and draft questions about celebrating Passover. Group members should interview someone of the Jewish faith about favorite childhood memories of Passover and whether he or she celebrates Passover in the same way today. Be sure to take notes.

Easter

A Season of Rebirth

DATE

Variable, the Sunday after the first full moon after March 21

NATURE OF HOLIDAY

Statutory, religious, traditional

OVERVIEW

The handout shows how the Christian holiday evolved out of a traditional spring-time celebration. Students may enjoy researching the legends or customs associated with this holiday. They could create a comparison chart or poster showing different springtime customs and foods in other lands.

Students may want to research the Easter story more thoroughly either individually or in groups. *The Story of Easter* by Aileen Fisher is one good resource. The list of topics suggested under Passover Research also apply to Easter since Passover and Easter are closely related. In fact, Jesus' last supper with his disciples may have been a Seder meal. Students who want to explore how these two holidays are related could begin by reviewing the overviews. They could then research holiday similarities and differences using an organizer similar to "New Year Celebrations around the World."

Easter Word Puzzle

Here is the answer key: 1. chocolate, 2. chick, 3. ribbon, 4. yellow, 5. buds, 6. robin, 7. Easter egg hunt, 8. lamb, 9. tulip, 10. duck, 11. Easter Monday, 12. daffodil, 13. nest, 14. colored, 15. hot cross buns, 16. rabbit, 17. Good Friday, 18. Eastre, 19. spring, 20. Easter lily, 21. Easter bonnet, 22. rebirth, 23. Easter bunny, 24. Easter eggs, 25. basket. The hidden message is: *Children like to find hidden Easter eggs.*

An Easter Tale

Ask students to write a story after they review the abbreviated version of the Easter folklore at the beginning of this student activity master. Options include comic strip and rebus formats. (See Christmas activities for information on rebus sentences.)

Who Stole the Easter Bunny?

Before the class writes this lighthearted Easter mystery, discuss what makes a story interesting and effective. Talk about plot, character, and the use of dialogue. A plot diagram may be helpful to plan stories. (Note: Older students enjoy writing this for younger children. They cast themselves in the role of the hero who solves the problem, defeats the villain and restores happiness to small children by finding the Easter bunny.)

Additional Activities

- Students could create a travel brochure on another country with pictures, flowers, symbols, legends and foods featured to "sell" that country as a travel destination in the spring. Travel brochures are often written on both sides of a page, with the page generally folded in three. This format could be adapted to suit the age and ability of the students.
- Suggest that students write concrete poems in the shape of an Easter symbol, such as an egg, rabbit, or chick.
- Invite students to research the use of eggs as works of art, e.g., Ukrainian or Fabergé, and present their reports in poster form.

Easter: *A Season of Rebirth*

Easter, like many other festivals, is a combination of an old festival with a Christian one. The holiday is named for the Teutonic, or Germanic, goddess of spring, Eastre. Her name symbolized spring and the rebirth of nature. It seemed to be an appropriate name to keep for the Christian celebration of the Resurrection of Jesus Christ, who rose from the dead three days after being crucified.

Crosses and Colored Eggs

Easter is a moveable feast. It occurs on the Sunday after the first moon after March 21, the spring equinox. It can be as early as March 22 or as late as April 25. The holiday actually begins on Good Friday. This day is solemn as it marks Christ's death on a cross. The cross is a key symbol of the Christian religion. Good Friday and Easter Sunday are statutory holidays.

Some traditions, such as eating hot cross buns with white sugary crosses, are special to Christianity, but many hold true for a variety of cultures.

Easter eggs — One widespread symbol for new life is the egg. The Egyptians, Persians, Greeks, and Romans, as well as Christians of ancient times, exchanged colored eggs during spring celebrations. Today the fanciest eggs are those of the Ukraine where Easter egg painting is an art. Perhaps the most famous eggs were created by the Russian, Fabergé. He made fifty-three golden gem-covered eggs for the Russian czar, or emperor. Chocolate eggs were introduced just before the beginning of the nineteenth century. Today Easter egg hunts, where children search for hard-boiled colored or chocolate eggs, are held.

Easter bonnets — Buying or receiving new clothes is a common theme to almost all cultures at the beginning of spring. In the past, women wore beautiful flower and ribbon-covered hats on Easter Sunday.

Easter bunny — Why do we have an Easter bunny instead of an Easter hen? According to folklore, Eastre's favorite creature was a bird, but when it angered her she transformed it into a rabbit. German immigrants brought the legend of the beloved Easter bunny to North America. Their children made small baskets (like nests) to collect eggs left by the Easter bunny.

Easter parades — Special parades with beautiful floats (decorated cars) or antique automobiles are held in some cities.

Flowers — Flowers are a beautiful symbol of the splendor of the new season. The crocus, tulip, and daffodil are popular, but the white Easter lily is the holiday symbol.

Stuffed animals — Children in North America are often given plush toys for Easter. These chicks, lambs or rabbits are substitutes for live animals. In the past, when many people lived on farms, baby animals surrounded children at this time of year.

Easter Word Puzzle

Solve the puzzle. Then write the letters from the boxes in order in the spaces at the bottom of the page to discover the hidden message.

1. a candy made from cocoa ☐ _ _ _ _ _ _ _
2. a baby chicken _ ☐ _ _ _
3. a long narrow piece of material used for tying things _ ☐ _ _ _ _
4. the color of the centre of an egg _ _ ☐ _ _ _
5. young leaves or flowers before they open _ _ ☐ _
6. a red-breasted spring bird ☐ _ _ _ _
7. the search for eggs on Easter Sunday _ _ _ _ _ _ ☐ _ _ _ _ ☐ _
8. a young sheep ☐ _ _ _
9. a spring flower that first came from Holland _ _ _ ☐ _
10. a bird that swims on water and often quacks _ _ _ ☐
11. the last day of the Easter holiday ☐ _ _ ☐ _ _ _ ☐ _ _ _ _
12. a yellow flower that blooms in the spring _ _ _ ☐ _ _ ☐ _
13. a place where birds lay eggs ☐ _ _ _
14. hard-boiled eggs are usually dyed or _ _ _ _ _ _ ☐
15. these sweet buns are a favorite at Easter ☐ _ _ _ _ _ _ _ _ _ _ _
16. a small animal that has long ears and long back legs for hopping _ _ _ _ ☐ _
17. the first day of Easter holiday _ _ _ ☐ _ _ _ ☐ _ _
18. goddess of spring ☐ _ _ _ _ _
19. the season when we celebrate Easter _ _ _ _ ☐ _
20. the flower of Easter ☐ ☐ _ _ _ _ _ _ _ _
21. a special Easter hat _ _ ☐ _ _ _ _ _ _ _ _ ☐
22. things coming to life again _ ☐ _ _ ☐ _ _
23. the rabbit that brings children Easter eggs ☐ _ _ _ _ _ _ _ _ _ _
24. special eggs _ _ _ _ _ _ _ ☐ ☐ _
25. what Easter eggs are carried in _ _ ☐ _ _ _

A favorite activity:

_ _ _ _ _ _ _ _ _ _ _ _ _ _ _ _ _ _ _ _ _ _ _

_ _ _ _ _ _ _ _ _ _

An Easter Tale

Have you ever wondered why a bunny delivers Easter eggs? Eggs are usually associated with birds. There is an old story that explains why a bunny and not a bird delivers Easter eggs ...

The holiday Easter gets its name from the Teutonic goddess, Eastre, goddess of spring. Legend has it that Eastre got angry at her favorite bird and changed him into a hare. Supposedly this is why today eggs, which are a universal symbol of rebirth, are delivered by a rabbit. The story has many variations. Another version comes from the German immigrants to North America who told their children to make nests and place them in the forests. When the children discovered brightly colored eggs, they decided that hens could not have laid them. They believed a special rabbit brought them.

Write a tale about how and why Eastre transformed the bird into a hare or why the Easter bunny brings the colored eggs. Plan your story before you write it. Visualize the place where your story takes place and describe it for your readers. Think about the characters: what would Eastre look like? How would she think and act? What type of bird do you think the Easter bird was? Add other characters, spring animals and illustrations to make your story more interesting. Use the story planner to help organize your writing.

Story Planner

Title: _____

Where: _____

When: _____

Characters: _____

_____

_____

Why: _____

_____

Who Stole the Easter Bunny?

Use the following guidelines to help you write your story.

Title: _____

Problem: Someone has kidnapped the Easter bunny. The Easter eggs cannot be delivered unless the Easter bunny is found.

Where: _____

When: The day before Easter

Villain(s): _____

Motive (Why was the Easter bunny stolen?) _____

_____

_____

Detective(s): _____

Other Characters: _____

Use this space to think about your characters before you begin to compose your story.

Character's Name	Physical Characteristics	Personality Traits

Earth Day

Taking Care of Our World

DATE
April 22

NATURE OF HOLIDAY
Recent

OVERVIEW

This holiday, and the activities pertaining to it, affords an opportunity for students to become more conscious of the natural environment and their relationship with it.

Ask students to identify causes of pollution under the headings Air, Land, and Water. For example, factories and cars can cause air pollution; the dumping of garbage and hazardous chemicals can cause land pollution; and oil spills and soil erosion can cause water pollution. Encourage students to discuss possible solutions. They could work in pairs to present this information on posters, taking a global or a local perspective. If the latter, suggest that students actively involve themselves in projects of benefit to their communities or schools, for example, bringing reusable food containers and recycling paper.

Earth Day Community Check-up

Before students search for answers to the check-up, brainstorm to see what they already know. You might want to have small groups each take a question and pool responses later on.

Endangered Species Research Organizer

Ask students to gather information from library resources or the Internet on different endangered animals or plants using the organizer provided. Consult Recommended Resources for leads. Students' reports could be posted on the bulletin board under the title "Endangered Species" or bound into a class book.

Additional Activities

- Brainstorm with the class environmental problems that affect the world as a whole. For example: the loss of animal species, the loss of rain forests, the depletion of the ocean's resources. Ask the students to write a letter to the people of the earth in the persona of Mother Earth. In their letters, students should ask people to take better care of the earth. Advise students not to put their names on the papers, but to design a letterhead to help them recognize their letters. When the letters are complete, collect them in two batches — one from the left side of the class and one from the right. See that the letters collected from one side of the class are distributed at random to students in the opposite group. Ask students to reply to the letters they receive from Mother Earth. The replies may be given directly to the original senders or read aloud to the class.
- Invite students to write haiku and to illustrate their poems. See the activity sheet under Japanese New Year.
- Suggest that students design a brochure to encourage people to reduce, reuse and recycle. Ask that they include a logo and a slogan.
- Encourage students to write a plea for help and understanding from the point of view of a fish, tree, lake, bird, or other part of nature. Students could present their pleas orally to the class.
- Let students research a natural disaster such as an earthquake or a man-made disaster such as an oil spill and present it as either a written or an oral report.

Earth Day: *Taking Care of Our World*

The first Earth Day events took place on April 22, 1970. On that day, people all over the United States took part in activities to bring about a greater awareness of our environment and the fact that we must take care of it. Those activities included cleaning up neighborhoods and planting trees. Today people all over the world celebrate Earth Day by striving to make the world a healthier place for all of us. For us to be healthy, the land that grows our food, the water we drink and the air we breathe must also be healthy and free from pollution and poisonous chemicals.

Acting in the Local Community

Think about your own community. How much do you know about it? If you want a glass of water to drink, you turn on the tap and fill your glass or open a bottle of water purchased at a store. But where does that water come from? In some countries children must walk to a well or village pump to collect water which they have to carry home in a container. Sometimes, the water is muddy or has bugs or bacteria in it, but it might be the only source available for drinking. Sometimes, there is no well or pump so the water must be collected from a river, the same river where people bathe and do their laundry. Sometimes, water in North America gets contaminated. Occasionally people will be told to boil their drinking water or trucks may bring fresh water to a community. This often happens after a natural disaster such as a flood. Sometimes, poisonous chemicals that have been left on the land get into the water supply. People may be evacuated from their homes due to air pollution caused by a fire at a factory or a train derailment of dangerous chemicals.

Think of what *you* can do to protect our environment and make it a healthier place to live. You can take part in recycling programs where materials are reused rather than dumped in landfills. You can respect trees, sometimes called the lungs of the earth because they give out oxygen. You can plant trees and other plants to keep our air healthier. There are many other ways that you can help to protect the earth.

Earth Day Community Check-up

Complete the chart for your community or neighborhood.

Community: _____

	Location	Any problems? What are your suggestions to protect the environment or help solve these problems?
Source for drinking water/ tap water		
Where does garbage go?		
Is there a recycling program?		
Sources of air pollution		
Where are the green spaces and parks?		
Where are the rivers, lakes and streams?		

When you have completed your chart, answer the following questions.

a) Which is the best feature of your community? _____

b) Which feature most needs improvement? _____

What suggestions do you have to bring about this improvement?

_____

Endangered Species Research Organizer

Choose an endangered species, such as the snow leopard. Research it in the library or on the Internet and complete the organizer below. Write a poem or story about your plant or animal. Try to make readers aware of the seriousness of its problem.

Name: _____	Endangered animal or plant:
Partner: _____	Species name:

Picture	Description
How many are there left?	**Why is it endangered?**

What might happen if it were to become extinct?	**What is being done to help this species?**

Cinco de Mayo

A Day of National Pride

DATE

May 5

NATURE OF HOLIDAY

Historical — Mexican; also celebrated by Hispanic peoples in the United States

OVERVIEW

To recognize one of the Hispanic cultures in the United States we have included the holiday that marks the Mexican Battle of Puebla, known simply by its date "Cinco de Mayo." Cinco de Mayo has become a popular time for parades, mariachi music, folk dancing and fiestas in the United States as well as Mexico. In fact, it is becoming a larger celebration in the States than in Mexico. Its study exposes students to a type of holiday with which they may be unfamiliar.

Students are asked to identify the 5Ws to ensure comprehension and gain a background for the projects.

Cinco de Mayo Crossword

The words used in this puzzle are presented in the overview. Students may need to refer to it while working on the puzzle.

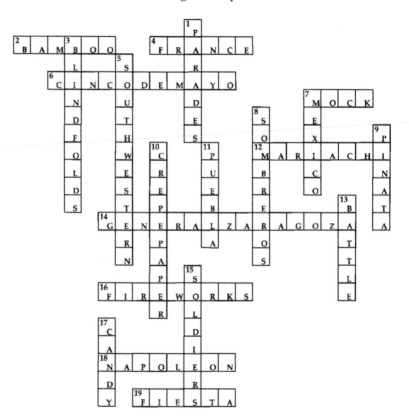

Cinco de Mayo Projects

A variety of projects are suggested on the student activity master. Students are encouraged to write or act imaginatively. The interview may require library research to provide background information. If you would like to build a piñata, we suggest using large sturdy balloons rather than clay pots or bamboo as a base for making the piñata. These are available at most art supply outlets. Instructions on how to make a piñata are provided in many art activity books.

The Cinco de Mayo Sombrero contest is included for fun as well as language development.

Cinco de Mayo: *A Day of National Pride*

Cinco de Mayo celebrates the emergence of the Mexican identity. It is celebrated in Mexico and in parts of the United States too. On May 5, 1862, the Mexican army  under General Zaragoza defeated a much larger French army in a battle at the small city of Puebla. France had loaned Mexico a lot of money. The trouble arose when Napoleon III of France needed money to  fight his wars in Europe and wanted the money repaid. Although this wasn't the end of the war (the French didn't leave for another five years), it was a spectacular win and morale booster for the people of Mexico.

Re-enacting a Battle

Cinco de Mayo is a happy, exciting day. Parades are common and mock battles, with people dressed as Mexican or French soldiers, re-enact the event. It is noisy, but safe as no real bullets are used. Soldiers die when they run out of blank ammunition. The most favorite role is that of General Zaragoza, who always wins!

Children, wearing blindfolds, take turns hitting candy-filled piñatas with a long stick. A piñata is a clay pot or bamboo frame covered with paper-mache and topped with frilly, colorful crepe paper. Most are animal shaped. When the piñata breaks all the children rush to gather the fallen candies.

In the evening there is a big party, or fiesta. Mariachi musicians, wearing large sombreros and dressed in traditional costumes, play music. People dance and sing after dinner. Later fireworks, often in animal, bird or fountain form, bring the festive occasion to an end.

In point form, summarize the information given above about Cinco de Mayo.

Who	What	Where	When	Why

Cinco de Mayo Crossword

ACROSS
2. a reed-like plant that is very strong, but can also be flexible
4. the country Mexico was fighting
6. May 5; a Mexican holiday (three words)
7. fake; not real
12. a member of a Mexican band
14. the leader of the Mexican army (two words)
16. these light up the sky
18. a famous French leader
19. a festive Spanish party

DOWN
1. happy processions through streets on holidays
3. eye covering that prevents sight
5. Mexico borders on this part of the U.S.
7. the country to the south of the U.S.
8. distinctive wide-brimmed Mexican hats
9. an animal-shaped, candy-filled children's party toy
10. colorful frilly paper; used for decorations (two words)
11. the place where the French and Mexicans fought on May 5, 1862
13. a fight between people
15. people who fight in an army
17. sweets

Cinco de Mayo Projects

Pick a project to complete by yourself or with a partner. (Check with your teacher.)

Poster or ad: Design an illustrated poster, advertisement, collage or brochure for a Cinco de Mayo festival. Include where, when, and what events will be held.

Biography: Pretend you are a reporter at Puebla, Mexico, on the evening of May 5, 1862. You are interviewing General Zaragoza. Present your interview as a skit (you need a partner to be the general) or write it as a newspaper article. You might also want to add other characters such as Mexican soldiers, parents of soldiers, French soldiers or townspeople.

Piñata poems: Write an animal, bird or star/moon/sun shape poem. Write a good copy on colorful paper. Place all poems on a bulletin board, or fill a piñata with small candies and the poems. Have a piñata party! With adult supervision, take turns trying to hit and break the piñata.

Cinco de Mayo Sombrero

How many words, both English and Spanish, can you create from the letters of the word *sombrero*? Use a dictionary to check your spellings.

English	Spanish

General Celebration Activities

Many of the activities listed under specific holidays can be used directly or are easily adapted to almost all celebrations. Some additional activity masters designed to help put holidays into context follow.

National Birthdays

Some students are recent immigrants and others know people who are. This organizer allows the students to write about a national day by using personal experience, interviews and library research. We have provided questions rather than topic headings in order to encourage interviews.

Activities for National Birthdays

For anyone wishing to explore a national holiday in more depth, this activity master suggests a variety of focused research projects and creative writing. It also offers several opportunities for brainstorming. It applies best to Canada Day and Independence Day.

Celebrating Our Heritages: Totem Poles

This activity would work particularly well at the beginning of the school year as a way for students to introduce themselves to their classmates. Show students pictures of totem poles and discuss how they tell the story of a family. Brainstorm common characteristics of animals. For example: eagle = power; swan = grace. For younger students, you will probably want to simplify the detailed instructions. (Totem pole size is up to you: we use an 8½" x 11" sheet.)
Extension: Ask students to research or read a Native myth and retell or present it to the class as a play, poster, poem, or report.

Calendars

The activity masters for New Year celebrations refer to calendars and may spark an interest in them. Doing this group research could be combined with a science or social studies unit. Discuss with students how they can present their projects. The medicine wheel and the zodiac need to be drawn. Encourage the students to give an oral report.

The Year; The Months of the Year

This organizer is intended to stimulate thought about the year. Once students have completed it, they can refer to the next complementary one to write a poem about the months of the year. Another idea is to complete details about each month as it occurs, with students writing about the summer either in September or June. Students can also use "The Year" to keep track of when celebrations occur and can store this in their portfolios. When the organizer is finished, they will have a calendar of holidays they have celebrated.

Symbols

If students understand the significance, or meaning, of a symbol, then they have acquired a greater understanding of a celebration. This organizer can be used for pre- or post-evaluation. It asks students to match the symbol with the celebration. Several conclusions will become apparent to students, perhaps the most important being that there is considerable similarity in cultural celebrations throughout the world. When students place a symbol for a celebration on the world map, there may not necessarily be a correct answer. Many celebrations are a blending of traditions.

Idioms Brought to Life

First, discuss with students what idioms are. Brainstorm ideas for the holiday being studied. Invite students to work in pairs to discuss the worksheets. When students have come up with some idioms, ask them to present them to the class. You might want to collate a class booklet for each holiday or ask students to create portfolios in which they keep all of their holiday materials.

Holiday Idioms

You can use this comparative chart either before studying celebrations in order to find out what students already know or as a follow-up activity to see what they have learned. You can make up similar sheets for other celebrations, if desired.

Words of Wisdom

Students explore a proverb or famous quotation in three ways: definition, sentence and art. An excerpt from a speech by Martin Luther King, Jr., would work particularly well here.

Wishing We Were There

This student activity master encourages students to identify with someone taking part in a celebration. Students work with conditionals: future possible, present unreal, and past unreal. They then have an opportunity to write a "What if" poem.

The last three student activity pages facilitate exploration of celebrations through literature such as is listed under Recommended Resources.

Plan Your Own Celebration

Students may enjoy creating their own celebrations as an individual or as a group activity. They can also apply the activity master to any special local celebrations in which they take part. The exercise reminds them that celebrations have much in common.

Story Map and Timeline

This organizer allows students, especially Grade 6 and above, to clarify their understanding of the elements of a novel.

Chapter Log

While reading a novel, students can use this sheet to explore characters, symbols, new words, and key events in each chapter.

Ways of Responding to Books

This handout provides a wealth of creative ideas on responding to a novel. These range from designing a book jacket to acting out a favorite scene with puppets.

National Birthdays

Research the national day of your country or that of a neighboring country. Interview someone from that country or research the holiday in the library or on the Internet.

This planner will help you to record and organize the information.

Questions	Replies or Answers
What is the name of the country?	
What is the date of its birthday?	
What is the name of the celebration?	
Is it a statutory holiday? (Do most people have the day off?)	
Are there official celebrations on this day? What happens? Are there official parties?	
Is there a parade?	
Are there any fireworks?	
Do people wear special costumes?	
What types of foods are eaten on this day?	
What do people do on this day to make it special?	
If you are interviewing someone or drawing on your own experience, how do they/you celebrate this day?	
Is there a story about this day? If so, what?	
Find, draw or describe the national flag. Is there a story behind the origin?	
What is the national anthem? Is it played on this day?	
What are the national symbols, sports or activities?	
What other things make this day special?	

Using the replies or answers prepare a write-up for your class.
Discuss with your teacher and class how it should be presented.
Here are some possibilities:
- Make posters: Include artwork, flags, pictures, as well as the information you found. If possible, bring native artifacts to school.
- Design a brochure or an invitation card to invite people to a birthday party for the country.
- Prepare an advertising slogan for this day.
- Design a wordsearch, crossword puzzle, or word spiral for this day. First, choose 10 to 20 important words. Then create the puzzle.

Combine all of the reports into a book/display that could be called "Our Countries' Birthdays" or just "Our Heritage Days." Perhaps you could pick one day on which to celebrate all of the birthdays together and organize a birthday party for it.

Activities for National Birthdays

Flags

Research the national flag: What is its story? What do flags stand for? When do we fly flags? When do we lower them? How should we treat or handle them?
Design your own personal flag: Give a key to explain the symbols and colors you have chosen and the meaning of your flag. Present your flag to the class and tell your classmates about it.

Anthems

Write out the words to your national anthem—"O Canada" or "The Star Spangled Banner." Illustrate it with the flag or a collage of national scenes. Do you know any other songs that describe the country? What are they?

Travel Brochures

I am a stranger to your country, but I would like to visit it. Tell me what is special about it, what I should see, where I should go ...
Respond to this letter fragment or, using maps and other brochures, create an advertising brochure promoting your country or a neighboring one.

Symbols

Research national animals, for example, the beaver for Canada, or national birds, such as the bald eagle for the United States.

Create a puzzle poem or riddle based on a national symbol for other students in the class. For example:

> *Who am I?*
> *On Canada's first stamp you'll find me,*
> *although fur traders hunted me almost till extinction.*

Famous People

If you had the opportunity, what famous citizen would you like to talk to? That person might be someone from history, such as Sir Wilfrid Laurier, prime minister of Canada, or Abraham Lincoln, president of the United States. Or, you could choose someone alive today, such as astronaut Roberta Bondar or undersea explorer Robert Ballard. With a partner, research and write an interview with the person you admire. Present your interview to the class. Perhaps the interview could be videotaped. Here are some suggestions:

Explorers: John Cabot, Canada; Robert Edwin Peary, U.S.
Inventors: Alexander Graham Bell, Canada/U.S.; Thomas Edison, U.S.
Scientists: Sir Frederick Banting, Canada; Benjamin Franklin, U.S.
Athletes: Wayne Gretzky, Canada; Tiger Woods, U.S.
Musical Performers: Céline Dion, Canada; Bob Dylan, U.S.
Visual Artists: Emily Carr, Canada; John James Audubon, U.S.
Authors: L. M. Montgomery, Canada; Ursula Le Guin, U.S.

Celebrating Our Heritages

Totem Poles

Totem poles are one of the main symbols of the coastal Indians of western North America. Their history is fascinating, for every totem pole tells a story.

People knew who someone was by looking at their totem pole. Totems were a way of recording pictorially the history of a family or clan. Animals, plants, symbols and human figures important to the family would be intricately carved on the post, which would then be painted in bold colors and erected before the family longhouse. The animals used on a pole reflected the characteristics of that clan.

Design a totem pole to tell people who *you* are! Include pictures that reveal your heritage or family history, the groups you are a part of, as well as your personal interests. Choose an animal to represent you and include this animal as a part of your totem.

This list may help you to think about what to include. Brainstorm with your class or group additional symbols.

Country	Province/State	City	School	Family	You
• Flag • National animal, flower, motto • National sports • National symbols • National heroes	• Flag • Flower • Symbols • Special places • Industries • Important points, events	• City flag • Symbols/logos • Special places • What people think of when they hear the name of your city or town	• School logo • Mascot • Flower • Important things about your school • Clubs, sports, etc. • Other groups	• The flags of the countries of your ancestors • Special symbols • Pictures of your family • Special foods	• Your picture • Hobbies • Pets • Favorite foods • Favorite clothes • Sports

At the top of your totem pole draw a picture of yourself, as it is *your* totem pole. You can create an overall shape such as that of a bird with the picture of yourself as the head, the national flag as the neck, and other flags/logos as wings. Everything else would be a part of the body and drawn below. Color your totem.

Present your totem pole to the class. Write the story of your totem in prose (like a story) or verse (poem). Tell your class the story as you show your totem. Display the totem poles and write-ups in the classroom or school.

Calendars

How do we know how long a year is? a day? an hour? Why do we have leap years? Where do we get the names of our days? our months? Why is a month called a month? Do you think of time as a line or as a circle? Time, and keeping track of the passage of time, has been something that has fascinated humanity throughout the ages. Various cultures have sometimes found different (and sometimes similar) answers to these questions.

Break into small groups and research a type of calendar. Present your research to the class in a way that is appropriate to the topic. For example, the zodiac or the medicine wheel would lend itself to poster creation. You might also consider making a brochure, flyer, model or chart.

Solar calendars
Lunar calendars
Luni-solar calendars
Native American calendar — the medicine wheel
Zodiac
Origins of the names of the days and the months (English, French)

Use the following organizer to record notes on your topic.

Topic: _____

Names of the people in the group: _____

Where you found your information: (books, etc.)
_____
_____

Information notes:

Who	What	Where	When	Why

Any additional information: _____

The Year

In the organizer below write ideas about each month. Outline the weather, the temperature, people's activities or feelings, the clothes they might wear, and the happenings in nature (animals, plants).

January	February
March	April
May	June
July	August
September	October
November	December

The Months of the Year

Write a poem on the months of the year. You can use the organizer "The Year" to prepare for your poetry writing. For each month write two lines. Transfer your poem to another paper and illustrate.

January _____
_____

February _____
_____

March _____
_____

April _____
_____

May _____
_____

June _____
_____

July _____
_____

August _____
_____

September _____
_____

October _____
_____

November _____
_____

December _____
_____

Symbols

We recognize a holiday or celebration by its symbols, the things, objects or colors that come to mind when we think about the holiday. Symbols form a big part of everyday life. For example, the dove represents, or stands for, peace. We understand and remember an event if we know its symbol.

What symbols do you know? Place the names of the symbols listed below under the name(s) of the celebration they represent. Angels, baby, balloons, black, black cats, bonhomme, bow and arrow, cake, candles, candy cane, cards, chocolates, costumes, Cupid, dipas, dove, dragon, earth, eggs, Father Time, firecrackers, flag, games, gifts, green, groundhog, hearts, holly, horn of plenty, horns, jack o' lanterns, Janus, kites, lace, lights, loud bells, magi, maple leaf, mistletoe, Moses, Mother Earth, nativity, new baby, noise makers, pine, poppy, pumpkins, rabbit, red, red envelopes, resolutions, Santa, seder, shamrock, silence, sombrero, piñata, St. Patrick, stars, stockings, treats, trees, tricks, turkey. What other symbols do you know?

Thanksgiving	Diwali	Remembrance/ Veterans Day	Christmas	New Year (any)	Groundhog Day	St. Patrick's Day	Kwanzaa
St. Valentine's Day	Easter	Passover	Eid ul-Fitr	Earth Day	National Birthday	Personal Birthday	Cinco de Mayo

You might want to choose one symbol from each celebration and draw it on a world map on the country of origin of the holiday. Place the map in a writing or celebrations portfolio.

Idioms Brought to Life

Most holidays have idioms, or peculiar uses of language, associated with them. For example, when we make a New Year's resolution to study more or to be kinder to others, we are promising to *turn over a new leaf*. Discuss with your class or with a partner the idioms or expressions that are typical for the holiday you are celebrating. Choose one idiom and then bring it to life: First, explain its meaning; next, create a cartoon or picture illustration; and finally, write a short story to go with the picture. Use the idiom in your story.

Idiom:

_____

Meaning:

_____

_____

Cartoon or picture:

_____

Story:

_____
_____
_____
_____
_____
_____
_____
_____

Holiday Idioms

Most holidays have idioms, or special expressions of language, to go with them. Draw a picture to illustrate each idiom provided. Can you think of any other idioms that relate to these holidays? Choose one idiom to base a poem on and write the poem on a separate paper.

Thanksgiving	Hallowe'en	Remembrance/Veterans Day	Christmas
You reap what you sow.	You look like you've seen a ghost!	Lay down your arms!	Don't be a scrooge!

New Year's Day	St. Valentine's Day	Easter	St. Patrick's Day
Wipe the slate clean.	Fall head over heels in love …	Don't put all your eggs in one basket.	Kiss the blarney stone.

Words of Wisdom

Proverbs are commonly accepted words of wisdom, or maxims. For example: It is better to give than to receive. By famous quotation, we mean something that an individual has said that has been remembered and adopted by other people. Franklin Delano Roosevelt's "The only thing we have to fear is fear itself" is such a quotation. Either work with the saying your teacher gives you or come up with one related to the holiday you are studying.

Saying:

Proverb ☐   Famous Quotation ☐   Who said it? _____

What does it mean?

Use it in a sentence.

Draw a picture to illustrate the saying.

Wishing We Were There

When we think about celebrations in other countries we often imagine what we would do if we were there. Think about the holiday you are studying. Try to put yourself in the "shoes" of someone who would be taking part in it and tell what you would do. For example, if you were in Japan, what would you be doing on New Year's Day? the day before? the day after? Use the three basic forms of conditionals.

Future Possible: what you will do if ...
Present Unreal: what you would do if ...
Past Unreal: what you would have done if ...

Future Possible:_____

Present Unreal:_____

Past Unreal: _____

Similarly, when we want something to be different from what it is, we express our ideas as *wishes*. Think about the holiday again and write three wishes.

A wish about the future:_____

A wish about the present:_____

A wish about the past:_____

Now that you have had a chance to think about what you would do, write your ideas in the form of a "What if" poem.

What if ...

_____
_____
_____
_____
_____
_____
_____
_____

Plan Your Own Celebration

Choose an event (perhaps a birthday or school or community happening) you would like to celebrate. Complete the following chart.

Event: _____

Name of celebration: _____

Reasons for choosing the event:

_____

_____

_____

Date: _____

Symbol:

Idiom or saying:

_____

_____

Activities:

_____

_____

_____

Special foods:

_____

_____

_____

Features unique to the celebration:

_____

_____

_____

Illustrate your celebration on a poster or make a flyer for it.

Story Map and Timeline

Book Title: _____

Circle the number of stars you would give this book: ★ ★ ★ ★

Fill in each box below with information about the novel you are reading.

Main characters:

Setting:

Problem:

Timeline:

Climax

Conclusion

Rising Action

Activating Circumstances

Introduction

Theme:

Chapter Log

Title: _____

Author: _____ Pages: _____

Chapter: _____

Characters	Major/Minor	Descriptive Adjectives (at least three)	What are they like? How do you know this?

Symbols and Their Significance	What happened?

An Important Sentence	Five New Words and Meanings	New Verbs

Ways of Responding to Books

After you have read a book on a holiday theme, rate it using a four star system: 4 stars = excellent, 3 = very good, 2 = OK, 1 = fair, 0 = don't waste your time reading it. Then complete *one* of the following:

- Explain how your story tells about the culture of a country or about a celebration.
- Interview the main character for a TV program. (You will need a partner for this.)
- Draw a map showing the places in the story.
- Write an advertisement for the book.
- Write a book review for the radio. (This could be tape-recorded.)
- Pick your favorite scene from the story. Design or make puppets and have the puppets act out the scene. (Suggestions for puppets: paper bag puppets, cardboard cutouts, sock puppets, finger puppets.)
- Draw and color a portrait of your favorite character.
- Rewrite the ending of the story. Or, outline a sequel for the book.
- Write a poem about the story.
- Draw a sociogram for the book. Include important characters, use arrows to show interaction, and show locations and significant objects.
- Design a book jacket:
    Front — Draw a picture to make the reader want to read the book.
    Back cover — Make up a short review of the book.
    Front inside flyleaf — Write a short summary of the plot, but do not tell everything.
    Back inside flyleaf — Give highlights of the author's life or other books.
- Make a story map, timeline or flow chart for the book.
- If the book presents a two-sided problem, set up a debate with other students.
- Create a cartoon based on the story. Cartoons are exaggerated pictures and words are often used as symbols. (Be sure to include thought or speech bubbles.)

Recommended Resources

This list reflects some of the titles we know and would like to bring to your attention. It is not intended to be comprehensive. You are sure to have favorites that are excellent, but do not appear here.
*Reference books

General Books Relevant to Celebrations

*Foster, John. *Let's Celebrate: Festival Poems*. Oxford, U.K.: Oxford University Press, 1989.

*Laughlin, Mildred, and Kathy Latrobe. *Readers Theatre for Children*. Englewood, CT: Teacher Ideas Press, 1990.

*Mossman, Jennifer, ed. *Holidays and Anniversaries of the World*. 2d ed. Detroit: Gale Research, 1989.

*Parry, Caroline. *Let's Celebrate: Canada's Special Days*. Toronto: Kids Can Press, 1984.

*Thompson, Sue, and Barbara Carlson. *Holidays, Festivals and Celebrations of the World*. Detroit: Omnigraphics, 1994.

Thanksgiving

Bunting, Eve. *A Turkey for Thanksgiving*. Boston, MA: Houghton Mifflin, 1995.

Capote, Truman. *The Thanksgiving Visitor*. New York: Alfred A. Knopf, 1996.

Lewicki, Krys. *Thanksgiving Day in Canada*. Toronto: Napoleon, 1995.

Hallowe'en

Ray, Mary Lyn. *Pumpkins*. New York: Harcourt Brace, 1992.

Ray, David. *Pumpkin Light*. New York: Philomel Books, 1993.

Sendak, Maurice. *Where the Wild Things Are*. New York: Harper & Row, 1963.

El Dia de los Muertos (Spanish holiday; expands multicultural aspect of Hallowe'en)

Ancona, George. *Pablo Remembers: The Fiesta of the Day of the Dead*. New York: Lothrop, Lee & Shepard Books, 1993.

Hoyt-Goldsmith, Diane. *Day of the Dead*. New York: Holiday House, 1994.

Remembrance Day/Veterans Day

Coerr, Eleanor B. *Sadako*. New York: Putnam Publishing Group, 1995.

Foreman, Michael. *War Game*. London, U.K.: Pavilion Books, 1993.

Granfield, Linda. *In Flanders Fields: The Story of the Poem by John McCrae*. Toronto: Stoddart Kids, 1995.

Eid ul-Fitr

Ghazi, Suhaib. *Ramadan*. New York: Holiday House, 1996.

*Lawton, Clive A. *Celebrating Islam*. Wiltshire, U.K.: Young Library Ltd., 1994.

Diwali

Beach, Milo C. *The Adventures of Rama*. Washington, D.C.: Freer, 1983.

*MacMillan, Dianne R. *Diwali: Hindu Festival of Lights*. Springfield, N.J.: Enslow, 1997.

Christmas

Brimner, Larry. *Merry Christmas, Old Armadillo*. Honesdale, PA: Boyds Mills Press, 1997.

Cooper, Susan. *The Dark Is Rising*. New York: Simon & Schuster Children's, 1973.

Kurelek, William. *A Northern Nativity: Christmas Dreams of a Prairie Boy*. Toronto: Tundra, 1984.

Lunn, Janet. *One Hundred Shining Candles*. Toronto: Lester & Orpen Dennys, 1990.

Robinson, Barbara. *The Best Christmas Pageant Ever*. New York: HarperCollins Children's Books, 1972.

Say, Allen. *Tree of Cranes*. Boston, MA: Houghton Mifflin, 1991.

Kwanzaa

Aardema, Verna. *Traveling to Tondo*. New York: Alfred A. Knopf, 1991.

Burden-Patmon, Denise. *Imani's Gift at Kwanzaa*. New York: Simon & Schuster Childen's, 1993.

Chocolate, Deborah Newton. *Kwanzaa*. Chicago: Children's Press, 1990.

De Sauza, James. *Brother Anansi and the Cattle Ranch*. San Francisco, CA: Children's Book Press, 1989.

Hill, Lawrence. *Trials and Triumphs: The Story of African-Canadians*. Toronto: Umbrella Press, 1993.

Lottridge, Celia Barker. *The Name of the Tree*. Toronto: Groundwood, 1989.

Mollel, Tololwa M. *The Orphan Boy*. Toronto: Oxford University Press, 1990.

Pinsey, Andrea Davis. *Seven Candles for Kwanzaa*. New York: Dial Books for Young People, 1993.

Porter, A. P. *Kwanzaa*. Minneapolis: Carolrhoda Books, 1991.

New Year

Bear, Magdalen. *Canadian Days*. Markham, ON: Pembroke, 1990.

Bernhard, Emery. *Happy New Year*. New York: Dutton Children's Books, 1996.

Korean New Year

Climo, Shirley. *The Korean Cinderella*. New York: HarperCollins Children's Books, 1993.

Hyun, Peter, ed. *Korea's Favorite Tales and Lyrics*. Boston, MA: Charles E. Tuttle Co., 1986.

Japanese New Year

Japan. (*Fiesta* series) Danbury, CT: Grolier Educational, 1997.

Galef, David. *Even Monkeys Fall from Trees: And Other Japanese Proverbs.* Boston, MA: Charles E. Tuttle Co., 1987.

Martin, Rafe. *Mysterious Tales of Japan.* New York: Putnam Publishing Group, 1996.

Snyder, Dianne. *The Boy of the Three-Year Nap.* Boston, MA: Houghton Mifflin, 1993.

Yagawa, Sumiko. *The Crane Wife.* Magnolia, MA: Peter Smith, 1992.

Chinese New Year

Chinn, Karen. *Sam and the Lucky Money.* New York: Lee & Low Books, 1995.

*Stepanchuk, Carol. *Mooncakes and Hungry Ghosts*: *Festivals of China.* San Francisco: China Books, 1991.

Stepanchuk, Carol. *Red Eggs and Dragon Boats: Celebrating Chinese Festivals.* Berkeley, CA: Pacific View Press, 1994.

Wallace, Ian. *Chin Chiang and the Dragon's Dance.* Toronto: Groundwood, 1992.

Martin Luther King, Jr., Day

Adler, David. *A Picture Book of Martin Luther King, Jr.* New York: Holiday House, 1990.

Archibald, Jo-Ann, and Val Friesen, eds. *Courageous Spirits: Aboriginal Heroes of Our Children.* Penticton, B.C.: Theytus Books, 1993. (Book plus TG)

Darby, Jean. *Martin Luther King, Jr.* Minneapolis: Lerner, 1990.

Hakim, Rita. *Martin Luther King, Jr., and the March Toward Freedom.* Brookfield, CT: Millbrook Press, 1991.

Winter Carnival (and Other Carnivals)

Dorros, Arthur. *Tonight Is Carnival.* New York: Dutton Children's Books, 1995.

Groundhog Day

Kroll, Steven. *It's Groundhog Day!* New York: Holiday House, 1987.

Sikundar, Sylvia. *Windows on the World.* Vancouver: Pacific Educational Press, 1996.

St. Valentine's Day

Barth, Edna. *Hearts, Cupids and Red Roses: The Story of the Valentine Symbols.* Boston, MA: Houghton Mifflin, 1982.

Bauer, Caroline, ed. *Valentine's Day: Stories and Poems.* New York: HarperCollins Children's Books, 1993.

Sabuda, Robert. *Saint Valentine.* New York: Simon & Schuster Children's, 1992.

Sharmat, Marjorie W. *Nate the Great and the Mushy Valentine.* New York: Dell, 1995.

St. Patrick's Day

Gibbons, Gail. *St. Patrick's Day*. New York: Holiday House, 1995.

Passover

Goldin, Barbara D. *The Passover Journey: A Seder Companion*. New York: Viking, 1994.
Lawton, Clive. *Celebrating Jewry*. Wiltshire, U.K.: Young Library Ltd., 1994.

Easter

Fisher, Aileen. *The Story of Easter*. New York: HarperCollins Children's Books, 1997.
Polacco, Patricia. *Rechenka's Eggs*. New York: Putnam Publishing Group, 1996.

Earth Day

Caduto, Michael, and Joseph Bruchac. *Keepers of the Earth*. Saskatoon: Fifth House, 1989.
Caduto, Michael, and Joseph Bruchac. *Keepers of the Animals*. Saskatoon: Fifth House, 1991.
Cherry, Lynne. *The Great Kapok Tree*. New York: Harcourt Brace, 1990.
*Dwyer, Jim. *Earth Works: Recommended Fiction and Non-Fiction about Nature and the Environment*. New York: Neal-Schuman, 1995.
Facklam, Margery. *And Then There Was One*. New York: Little, Brown & Co., 1993.
Rose, Deborah L. *People Who Hugged the Trees*. Boulder, CO: Rinehart, Roberts, 1994.
*Sheehan, Kathryn, and Mary Waidner. *Earth Child: Songs and Stories about Living Lightly on the Planet Earth*. 2d rev. ed. Tulsa, OK: Council Oak Books, 1995.

Cinco de Mayo

Behrens, June. *Fiesta!* Danbury, CT: Children's Press, 1978.

General Celebration Activities

Alderson, Sue Ann. *Pond Seasons*. Toronto: Groundwood, 1997.
Bruce-Mitford, Miranda. *The Illustrated Book of Signs & Symbols*. New York: DK Publishing, 1996.
Hughes, Paul. *The Days of the Week*. Ada, OK: Garrett Educational, 1989.

Language Skills Index

This skills index provides a cross-reference for locating specific skill topics. However, most activities are integrated using reading, writing, oral and listening skills.

5161